I0114451

# Fallen Walls and Fallen Towers: The Fate of the Nation in a Global World

by Adrienne Redd

NIMBLE BOOKS LLC

NIMBLE BOOKS LLC

Nimble Books LLC

1521 Martha Avenue

Ann Arbor, MI, U.S.A 48103

http://www.NimbleBooks.com

wfz@nimblebooks.com

+1.734-330-2593

Copyright 2010-2011 by Adrienne Redd

Version 1.0; last saved 2010-08-30.

Printed in the United States of America

ISBN-13: 978-1-934840-99-3

The paper used in this publication meets the minimum requirements of the American National Standard for Information Sciences—Permanence of Paper for Printed Library Materials, ANSI Z39.48-1992. The paper is acid-free and lignin-free.

# CONTENTS

# ACKNOWLEDGMENTS

Thanks to my husband for his love and engagement with both my dissertation and this book. I also owe gratitude to my daughter, who edited portions of both. And I must also thank my young son, for trying to understand why I was working all the time for the first years of his life and for his enthusiasm (not exclusively based on the promise of a puppy) when I claimed to be finished.

I feel affectionate gratitude for the diligence and attentiveness of my dissertation committee, Christine Ho, Jim Spickard, and Jeremy Shapiro, as well as for the gracious ease of Mark Juergensmeyer, my external examiner.

Of the many friends, family and colleagues who commented on my lines of inquiry, I would particularly like to thank Critt Jarvis, Vince Mondillo, Skip Leeds, Robert Engelhardt, Mary Butler, Peter Baumann, Eric and Alonna Smith, Gene Mater, and Swaminathan Subramaniam. Fred Zimmerman, the editor and publisher of this book, has also been a valuable sounding board. Bob Hires, Helen Mallon, Sethanne Howard, Gaurrav Kanal, Big Dave Amidon, Chuck Garrettson, Katie McDermott, Mark Safransky, Robert Skarloff, Jared Trush, Doreen Loury, David Morgan, and Jennifer and Daylin Leach also contributed energy and curiosity. And I would also like to thank all the Stengles.

A decade ago, I "met" Tsvi Bisk virtually when we each wrote a chapter for a book on utopian thought compiled by Art Shostak. Since then he has always been willing to trade ideas and encourage me. My colleagues, David Kreda and Ross Koppel have also been particularly supportive. I would also like to thank the faculty of Lehigh University, Fielding Graduate University, and Temple University, especially Shanyang Zhao, who has shared his thoughts and critiqued mine for more than a decade.

# PREFACE. MESSAGE TO THE NATION-STATE: EVOLVE OR DIE

Every generation endures upheavals and shock. However, the birth or reconfiguration of 31[1] nation-states from 1990 to 2010 is historically exceeded only by the wave of decolonization of developing countries after 1941.

That's not the only indication that major change is underway. Diplomatic relations, once frontal, and to some extent comprehensible, affairs, are now overshadowed by asymmetrical assaults on civilians and infrastructure. Forms of money, jobs, products, threats, and ideas, are all hemorrhaging across boundaries—over which nation-states have waning control. Furthermore, no one seems sure whether the rise of multinational corporate behemoths, shadowy gray marketeers, and metanational projects (such as the I.M.F., World Bank, E.U., W.T.O., NATO and the U.N.) will help or hinder global order and justice.

It has been about 360 years since the Thirty Years War ended with the signing of the Peace of Westphalia in 1648, an event many theorists use as the inception of the nation-state. These indicators all point to a massive and as-yet undefined social shift—perhaps even the demise of the nation-state, as we have known it.

In order to better understand the nature of social upheaval, I reviewed predictions in both popular and scholarly literature after the end of the Cold War. I found that these predictions could be categorized into four families.

One family of predictions from the early 1990s was that there would be little or no order as we entered the 21st century. This is called the "ethnic chaos" theory. This line of thinking includes the

---

[1] Enumerated in chapter two.

ideas of Harvard professor Samuel Huntington—that certain cultures and "civilizations" are fundamentally incompatible and will continue to "clash" with no resolution in sight. The message underlying this group of treatises is that Muslim extremists will never be able to get along with the G20 and the rest of the industrialized world.

A second set of warnings emphasizes increasingly empire-like domination and control, particularly by the United States. Standing military control abroad (along with state-building projects) has been advocated by some as an antidote to social breakdown driven by sectarianism, other ideological strife and ethnic conflict. Other thinkers have warned against overextension and arbitrary force that they predict will morally and financially bankrupt the U.S. and its allies in imperial projects.

The third family of explanations says that the desire to participate in the global economy will be the most compelling force shaping reorganization of world politics. A popular proponent of this line of thought is author and *New York Times* columnist, Thomas Friedman.

The fourth school of thought can be loosely grouped under "globalization theory." One of the most important predictions is the notion of "globality" by British sociologist, Martin Albrow. He wrote that the planet itself, particularly in its fragility and declining viability, would become the hub of political decisions and public political understanding. This fourth family of ideas is not a political stance so much as it is a search for patterns and call for sensitivity as local culture collide with global capitalism and shifting political exigencies.

These four are all "non-state" perspectives on how older political patterns may be shifting. Each identifies something *other than* the nation-state as the factor that will mold society at the highest level.

Reviewing hundreds of texts written between 1946 and 2008, I found that responses to a series of landmarks recommended the *nation-*

*state* and not a "non-state" explanation to describe best available structure for dealing with earth-shaking political changes. The texts responded to crises and turning points for nation-states, such as the Bosnian Wars, conflict between Israel and Hezbollah in 2006, Hamas's and Fatah's contention for the Gaza Strip, struggle between Tamil separatists and Sri Lanka, and the attacks of September 11, 2001, as well as the founding and strengthening of metanational authorities.

Emphasis on the nation-state in the public sphere was a fifth possibility barely considered by scholars trying to make sense of the disorder of the late 20th and early 21st century; but it was what emerged from public texts as the dominant view, even while writers expressed bitter disappointment about ways that the nation-state was falling down on the job.

Expectations for the enduring potential of the nation-state constituted the major finding of my doctoral dissertation—a project I started in order to make sense of these seeming harbingers. Since then, I have puzzled over how the nation-state can live up to the perception that it will and should remain the prevailing large-scale social structure—but needs to get better at what it has historically done.

To answer this question, I reviewed expectations that scholars and other thinkers have had for the nation-state. What, after all, is it supposed to be doing?

I identified properties that writers have attributed to the nation-state. Among these are sovereignty, boundedness, unity (in an ethic or cultural sense), and modernity, i.e. rational decision-making and other "values" of the industrial age. These functions are central to how the nation-state has evolved to meet public needs. At the same time, such properties are incompatible with new dimensions (both liberating and destabilizing) of globalization. An unstoppable torrent of money, people, things and ideas enabled by the removal of financial barriers, and by instantaneous communication and cheaper transportation may be breaking the international state-system. Yet I assert that it is the best system yet devised for negotiating the diverse and competing needs of increasingly multicultural populations.

I make a case that each of four historical functions must become both less absolute and more deliberate in the way that leaders and the public conceive of them. Sovereignty and control may need to be shared across boundaries, and will have important exceptions to the old expectation of strict noninterference.

Boundaries need to be precise yet credible—more carefully enforced for the flow of funding to terrorists, pathogens and weapons, but phased out for some things the nation-state should give up on trying to control, for both ethical and logistical reasons.

Ethnic or cultural unity as part of the conception of the nation-state is only destructive in public rhetoric and should be flagged and stamped out the way we have tried to stamp out hate speech. There are, however, other conceptions of nation-state unity that may be useful.

Finally, though some see it as destructive and fossilized, the phenomenon of *modernity* that catalyzed the first industrial revolution still has much to offer. It needs to be mined for what can help the nation-state function in an unregulated global system. The machinery of modernity needs to re-commit to long-term planetary viability rather than short-term efficiency and profit. It needs clarified rather than fragmented authority at the macroregional level. It must implement truly evenhanded application of rules, rather than lopsided protectionism. Jealous protection by established players (both governmental and corporate) of their narrow interests will ultimately hurt overall stability and well-being. This matters now, because we are all connected.

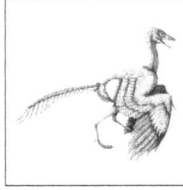

# CHAPTER ONE. THE OLD BIRD MUST EVOLVE

An upheaval in international relations. Examining public
discourse for hints about the trajectory of world order. Endurance of the nation-state. Four historical properties of the
nation-state must evolve: sovereignty, boundedness, unity,
and modernity.

Glued to a blond wood plaque in my office is a rough, gray chunk of
the Berlin Wall. When unrest began in divided Germany in late autumn of 1989, my friend Gene Mater, who had spent formative years
there, booked a flight to Berlin to see friends—thinking that Europe
east of the wall might be closed to westerners for months, or years.

After his arrival, Gene and his friends took part in the largest dem-
onstration in the history of the German Democratic Republic—a human chain or *Menschenkette* that stretched across the country from the
Baltic coast to the Czech border, and from the Iron Curtain to Frank-
furt-an-der-Oder, meeting in East Berlin. Events swung in the opposite
direction from what Gene had dreaded: the Wall was breached and
many less-controlled crossings became possible on November 9, 1989
as the world watched in stunned delight. Actual dismantling of the
Wall began on June 13, 1990 and continued through November 1991.

In late November, 1989, in the middle of the night my friend took a
hammer to the Wall on a dead-end street in West Berlin. He brought
back to me one of the small pieces he broke off.

That fragment of concrete continues to evoke for me the exhilaration of seeing the Berlin Wall come down. Until the autumn of 1989, I had never lived in a world that was not cut in two.

The Berlin Wall bisected a city, a nation-state, and the world. Its fall heralded enormous changes. Scholars and other thinkers are still debating what the collapse of the Wall and the dissolution of the U.S.S.R. mean to the nature of the nation-state and to our political future. Since then, more tectonic heaves have kept the world guessing.

These momentous changes inspired the research question that I discuss further in chapter two: in a nutshell, what is going on with world order? Is a macro social structure emerging or *re*-emerging to take the place of the nation-state? To interpret stunning political transformations (including the fall of the Berlin Wall, the implosion of the U.S.S.R. and subsequent Bosnian wars, and clashes involving non-states such as between Hezbollah-Israel and Hamas-Fatah) I tracked perception (measured by what words and metaphors employed) of macro social structures. Writers in the public sphere expressed overall disappointment with the nation-state's handling of six of the seven nation-state responsibilities that I identified. However, they also revealed the endurance of *state-centered discourse*, while implying a need for the evolution of some of the seven properties.

This book argues that to survive globalization the nation-state must evolve beyond the institution's early conception in the 17$^{th}$ century. Specifically, I urge society to collectively re-imagine the following four historical properties of the nation-state: sovereignty, boundedness, unity and modernity. I discuss these four and three other properties of the nation-state in greater detail below and in chapter four, where I recount the history and significance of the Treaties of Westphalia that began to codify the nation-state at the end of the Thirty Years' War.

First, absolute sovereignty—complete autonomy and self-determination of the nation-state—is unworkable in an interdependent community of states. Extreme examples of "islands" that have cut themselves off from the political mainland, such as North Korea and Myanmar, are compelling evidence of this.

Second, nation-states have neither the moral authority nor the resources to seal in or seal out flows of resources, information, or people. Nation-states will by necessity relax boundaries in some instances and seek better ways to impede truly toxic crossings (including contaminated consumer products, known criminals, and weapons or funding for terrorism). In other words, control over flows across national boundaries will need to be focused and implemented in a more selective way. Tools and inspections required to target disease vectors (like mad cow disease or H1N1 flu) may exemplify the changes that must take place in the conception and implementation of nation-state boundedness. If they are not carrying sickness or bombs, the nation-state cannot and *should* not try to stop people from merely seeking employment if they are from the "other side."

Third, public leaders need to choose between two contradictory conceptions of national unity. Leaders should promote unity of purpose and commitment to a given nation-state's shared vision of prosperity and equality under the law. Clearly, the mythology of national identity based in ethnic heritage predates the upheavals of accelerating globalization. However, the uncertainties of globalization have re-inflamed this error in the conception of the nation-state. In order to accrue power to themselves, demagogues have incited ethnically based genocide by encouraging people to stress the differences between themselves and outsiders. Horrendous (and artificial) social construction of racialized differences include those between Muslims and Hindus in India and elsewhere, between Sunnis and Shi'as, between and Anglo and Latino Americans. Our language in the free world has matured to fight racism and sexism. Similarly, calling attention to destructive mythology and directing opprobrium against the idea of the ethnically pure nation-state will takes us in a healthier direction. Even if free speech protections prohibit explicitly banning divisive language, there is much we can do with awareness of language alone. And if we don't re-frame the nation, we will suffer from murderous consequences.

Fourth, the modernity of the nation-state still holds enormous potential for settling disputes and addressing social problems. "Modernity" is a word that does not roll off the tongue, and many mistakenly use "modern" to mean "contemporary" or "technologically advanced." I explore the historical origins of modernity as an often assailed, but still valuable way of testing and legitimating knowledge. The major shift that emerged in the Renaissance and unfolded through the Enlightenment and Industrial Revolution is manifesting itself now as globalization: the torrent of people, problems, finances, and ideas across increasingly permeable borders. I assert that modernity's toolkit for establishing rules and sharing power is still the best game in town—but only if rule-makers and enforcers can re-commit to equitably administered constitutions, legislation, accords and conventions, while crafting a more resilient and sustainable nation-state.

## An Upheaval in International Relations

After 1989, for a time, unstoppable forces seemed to be uniting the world. And suddenly, only a few years later, and particularly after 2001, unstoppable forces seemed to be tearing the world apart. Writers from a range of backgrounds sounded alarms that well-established building blocks of international order (the nation-state being among the first casualties listed) appeared to be crumbling. This seemed apparent in the dissolution of Yugoslavia in the early 1990s; on September 11, 2001; in the war between Hezbollah and Israel across Lebanon's southern border in 2006; and the struggles between the flailing nation-states of Pakistan (and Afghanistan and multiple avatars of the Taliban). Not only have nation-states come apart at the seams over the past two decades, but non-states have clashed with non-states over territory supposedly controlled by nation-states. These and other confounding events of the past two decades seemed to show that the world was not converging as of the end of the Cold War, but falling apart.

The guesses about world order written after 1989 in hundreds of letters and editorials, and further discussion of world order in the public sphere revealed surprising motifs and themes.

In times of gravest crisis, it was the nation-state—not some other social structure—whether emergent or traditional—that was most commonly invoked as a source of potential stability and conflict resolution. Even so, some writers suggested that certain historical properties of the nation-state need to be re-imagined. The globalized world is outgrowing the nation-state *as it was originally conceived* in the treaty that ended the Thirty Years' War in 1648 and as it has endured through the age of nationalism and into the 20<sup>th</sup> century. At the same time, there are aspects of that dominant institution that are still useful.

Although my doctoral research did reveal the persistence of state-centered discourse, the past two decades have clearly also seen convulsions in political power arrangements. Chapter two asks: What is going on with world order? I review varying proposals from political science and the popular press that attempt to explain what (if anything) is happening to the world order. Some of the explanations turn on cultural identity (including religion) and tribal and ethnic conflict. Others foresee a shift away from the nation-state and a return to empire as the dominant social structure. Others emphasize metanational structures (like the European Union) or explore various branches of globalization theory.[2]

## Examining Public Discourse from 16 Public Intellectuals

My goal in chapter three is to convince the reader that "public discourse" is a meaningful idea in a fragmented, polarized storm of opposing views and media artifacts, and that the books, articles, and speeches of 16 diplomats, scholars, and authors support my recommended reconceptualization of the sovereignty, boundedness, unity, and modernity of the nation-state. In chapter three, I describe how and why I selected these 16 public intellectuals, define "public discourse," and explain how the writers' speeches and other texts offer insight into evolving concepts of the four relevant properties of the nation-state.

## Seven Nation-State Properties

In chapter four, I explain why I selected seven properties by which to measure the functioning of the nation-state. Namely:

- Sovereignty
- Nation-state boundedness
- Attribution
- Protection of and provision for social welfare

---

[2] "Globalization theory" is the label for writing that attempts to make sense of emerging dimensions of world interdependence and cultural mixing. British sociologist Martin Albrow's (1996) "globality" thesis falls under this aegis; it predicts that the planet itself will become the focus of political organization, rather than nation-states. For my doctoral research, I particularly focused on testing Albrow's thesis; it was only partially supported by my findings.

- Law and order
- Unity
- Modernity

There is substantial literature on "state failure," but how can "semi-failure" be understood? Since the nation-state is a complex, multidimensional entity that resists one-dimensional measurement, I needed sub-dimensions that I could readily track as people wrote about the nation-state. Thus, I selected these seven properties of the nation-state as a means of measuring writers' perceptions. I used discourse analysis to assess mentions of these properties in the newspaper texts. My findings were a surprise. Although writers saw nation-states (both in general and in specific cases) as failing to fulfill the seven functions, the overall perception was that the nation-state is not passé.

Chapter four surveys Enlightenment thought and work by the founding sociologist Max Weber; "state-centered" political theory (mostly written during the Cold War) and "postnational" prognostications. My survey shows that, from the days of early modern political philosophy through the most recent period, political order has been discussed in terms of fulfillment (or failure) of sovereignty, boundedness, attribution, protection of and provision for citizenry, lawfulness, unity, and modernity. In this book, I focus on the nation-state, but other social structures, such as metanational organizations and segment states, can also be thought of in terms of these properties.

## The Endurance of the Nation-State

I identified a set of turning points and crises from the 20th through the early 21st centuries to which letter and editorial writers responded. These events and processes included the founding of the United Nations (U.N.), North Atlantic Treaty Organization (NATO), European Union (E.U.), and World Trade Organization (W.T.O.), landmarks of the nuclear arms race, the rise and fall of the Berlin Wall, the collapse of the U.S.S.R., the Bosnian Wars, the dissolution of Yugoslavia, secession of Kosovo, and other selected independence movements, and selected actions of politically relevant non-states, like the Tamil separatists, Palestine liberation movement, al Qaeda, and Hezbollah. I found that, at the moments of direst crisis, contributors to *The New York Times*, *Times of India* and *Daily Gleaner* (of Jamaica) framed solutions in terms of the nation-state. The nation-state was foremost in their articulation of how to understand upheaval and change, and what to do about it.

In chapter five I explain my finding that, according to the hundreds of Indians, Americans, Caribbeans, Britons, Canadians, Pakistanis, Bangladeshis and others who wrote editorials and letters over the 62–year period I studied, the conventions and abilities of the historically imagined nation-state continue to be seen as the tools most likely to do the job at hand. Time and again, the writers recommended using the structures and procedures of the nation-state to try to negotiate and enforce differing goals and stances among players on the world stage and diverse populations.

Although current writers are committed to relying on the nation-state, it is worth recalling that the political order of the late Renaissance world had to be re-shaped for order to be maintained. Now, the nation-state must be re-thought in order to adapt and cope with the needs of a globe spinning ever faster. This book synthesizes suggestions from the editorial writers, my realizations as I reviewed writing about nation-state crises and turning points in the public sphere, and prescient and incisive writing by public thinkers to explore promising directions for the four properties of the nation-state that I identify as warranting re-thinking.

In chapter five, I explained how I found that, during some of the most bruising crises of the nation-state over the past two generations, opinion texts in the *New York Times*, *Times of India* and *Daily Gleaner* focused on ways in which nation-states should exercise leadership, broker peace agreements, include other (sometimes non-state) players in international dialogue and/or live up to their own stated rules. In other words, the accords, conventions, agreements, etc.—the substance of what I am calling "modernity"—are in place for many nation-states but writers criticized particular countries and countries in general for not adhering to their own standards (Aub 1992, Cohen 2009, *Daily Gleaner* 1973, Friedman 2005, *New York Times* 1968, *Times of India* 1982). These texts and others criticized the United States and India (home to two of the three newspapers), but also faulted the Soviet Union, Israel and other powers that violated their own public covenants of procedure, protection of rights, due process, adherence with international regulations, etc.

Though scholars and critics have long suggested the emergence of some other dominant social structure, in the data I examined, the nation-state continued to be perceived as preeminent. Does this mean that the state will continue to be the preeminent structure? Or that the writers are suffering from a failure of imagination? In other words, is there a new macro social structure emerging but leaders and thinkers don't recognize it yet? Or is it too difficult to locate in popular writing because there is not yet one agreed-upon term that refers to it?

Chapters three and six explain the methodological approach of the book. I argue that the 16 writers whose texts I examine are both bellwethers of and catalysts for further development of the nation-state after the series of major transformations and the pressures of globalization of the past few decades. This is consistent with the assertion by one of these writers, Jürgen Habermas:

With regard to the formation of modern states, mainly lawyers [and] diplomats engaged in the construction of an effective bureaucracy, while on the other side writers, historians, and journalists preceded the diplomatic and military efforts of statesmen (like Cavour and Bismarck) with the propagation of the—at first imaginary[3]—project of a nation unified on cultural terms. Both developments led to that European nation-state of the nineteenth century which in any case provides the context from with the present normative self-understanding of the constitutional state derives. (1996, p. 283)

Chapter three profiles the 16 thinkers and explains why I chose them. Chapter six summarizes the methods of the dissertation, explaining what discourse analysis is and how I counted words and synonyms in the editorial texts for the dissertation, and connects those methods to the current project.

## Re-Imagining Sovereignty

The nation-state was not initially conceived of as absolute, but leaders have ratcheted up their own prerogative to avoid being interfered with over the past century and a half. Given the complex interactions of the contemporary world, this primary property of the nation-state must be re-imagined for the nation-state to continue to function.

Nation-state sovereignty was originally developed as a solution to the overlapping authorities of the Catholic Church, other empires, independent cities, kingdoms, duchies, etc. of the late Middle Ages.

Although state sovereignty began as a barrier against overlapping claims of authority, the modern nation-state has engendered a new version of the late Medieval confusion, what Appadurai (2006) calls

---

[3] In sociology, "imaginary" means that collective agreements create social reality, *not* that these group perceptions (of abstractions like money, social affiliations, gender, race, etc.) are make-believe. See also Social Construction in the Glossary.

"entangled universalisms" that reach across state barriers. Ideas of the market, freedom, democracy, and human rights generated and advocated by avowedly autonomous nation-states have, ironically, become a justification for a new, super-absolute sovereignty in which arguments are advanced not only for not being governed by other nation-states but attempting to influence events beyond the homeland.

Clearly, the monolithic quality of the modern nation-state solved an administrative problem by concentrating more political power in one place—the nation-state. This has created the problem of the ungovernability of the individual state that Immanuel Kant worried about. Furthermore, with the interdependence engendered by globalization, there is another problem, which is that other members of the international community do not want to wait until a given states runs off the cliff of war, genocide, or environmental collapse before they respond. The solution to the contemporary equivalents of the overlapping claims of authority of the late medieval world is that nation-states must narrow rather than expand their claims on authority, to what is necessary to their survival.

In chapter seven, I discuss how the reconceptualization of sovereignty plays out in speeches, monographs, and other texts by the 16 intellectuals. Chapter seven also traces the history of the usage of "sovereignty" and examines ways in which it may be reconceived as shared, cooperative, or mutually conferred sovereignty.

## Re-Imagining Nation-State Boundedness

The re-imagining of sovereignty has been coming for a long time, but how to put that into action in terms of nation-state *boundaries* will require resourcefulness, courage and vision on the part of world leaders.

By globalization I mean the erosion of nation-state boundaries because of swift and inexpensive communications, and entangled destinies of the planet's inhabitants because of the global economy. Because of globalization, downturns in one locale are almost instantly felt around the world, and the pursuit of raw materials is depleting fish stocks, degrading arable soil, and contaminating clean water, as well as other necessary resources for human life.

Globalization is further defined in chapter eight, which explores the re-imagining of nation-state boundedness, in, and in the Glossary.

If sovereignty is *what* of the nation-state, then boundaries are the *how* and *where* of that sovereignty. If a state controls the people who reside within a national territory, plus the territory itself, then boundaries visually and practically define that control. Nation-states were originally imagined to have nearly complete control over their boundaries. Their armed forces controlled what happened inside the borders and boundaries, but were expected not to interfere with what was outside. Impermeable boundaries as a historical given of the nation-state also require reconsideration in an increasingly interdependent world.

## Re-Imagining Nation-State Unity

In chapter nine, I review and expand upon three suggestions from the German sociologist and philosopher Jürgen Habermas (one of the 16 public intellectuals) for dealing with the problem of imagining nation-state unity as cultural homogeneity. His first recommendation is to separate culture and state (as the framers of the American Constitution separated church and state), his second is to re-commit to a nation-state that helps to foster material well-being for its citizens, and the third is for public discourse to celebrate citizenship in the nation-state, but within a larger context of cosmopolitan membership and common good.

Let me say this more plainly. It has seemed to me for several decades that progressives are embarrassed of being patriotic—that the heartfelt, unabashed patriotism that conservatives express about their nation-states is not a pride liberals feel authentic or comfortable sharing. For all its failures in execution, for all the historical and ongoing injuries committed by my nation, I feel exhilaration in the promise of the U.S. Constitution and in the instances when it has functioned properly. As several of the public intellectuals reviewed suggest, I recommend celebration of the secular, particularity-blind proceduralism of the constitutional democracy, without regard to race, ethnicity, language or faith. Geeky stuff, but that's really what brings tears to my eyes. More leaders, more speakers in the public realm who celebrate the inclusive, multicultural nation-state and the potential for justice in the operating system of the nation-state would make for fewer genocides and a less divided society.

The classic conception of "unity" in America and some of the other immigration-based and revolutionary (like France) nation-states is of a shared, forward-looking vision. Ethnic unity is a shibboleth re-ignited by the misguided racism of Woodrow Wilson in his approach to the end of WWI and manipulated by other demagogues. This kind of ethnic nationalism won't work in a world where people stream back and forth across nation-state boundaries, as they mix, migrate, and interact with everyone within reach—by land, sea, air, and wired or wireless communication. As people are bombarded by "alien" and threatening influences, there needs to be a standard for inclusion based on will and choice, not ascribed characteristics like native language or heritage. The Mexican or Iranian who makes a life in a new country is more admirable in many ways than I am for my Revolutionary-era ancestry.

## Re-Imagining Modernity

Modernity, the fourth property of the nation-state, is the youngest and most contradictory. Theorists like political sociologist Benedict Anderson, author of the watershed work *Imagined Communities* (1983/2006), and modernist political theorists Eric Hobsbawm (1962, 1990) and Ernest Gellner (1997) argued that the nation-state grew to be an institution in lock-step with what I call "modernism"—that is, industrialism, short-term profit and other ideologies that have taken their human toll. Polish sociologist and philosopher Zygmunt Bauman and cultural anthropologist Arjun Appadurai (two of the 16 public intellectuals) have made trenchant observations regarding those aspects of the modernity of the nation-state and the modernity of globalization that they believe have become unworkable.

Chapter ten offers a short history of modernity, with the purpose of demonstrating that (1) modernity is inextricably bound with the nation-state, (2) it is here to stay, and (3) this is a good thing. By "modernity," I mean logic, the ability to disprove ideas that are wrong, and efficiency. I use the term "modernism" to refer to the negative aspects of this paradigm shift that have trampled human well-being, such as the unstoppable momentum of technology and the valuing of profit over people.

I use "modernity" to refer to the original historical shift more than 500 years ago *away* from authority and political structures enforced by ritual, dogma and intolerance of dissent. The late medieval world fell so hard because it had few ways to incorporate disagreement or creativity, without tearing existing institutions to the ground. That world shifted to political structures increasingly based on reason, consistent rule sets, and social contracts arrived at via empirical observation and trial and error. When Francis Bacon tested the hypothesis that life (maggots) spontaneously generated in meat, he did so by covering one piece and leaving one exposed for flies to lay their eggs. The covered meat did not spontaneously fill with larvae. The result of the rise of modernity has been a shift from knowledge based in authority to knowledge based in testing and the ability to determine that earlier hypotheses are false and should be discarded. I am not saying that the modern world is always rational. I am say that it has a set of tools for integrating change that the *ancien régime* did not.

The shift to modernity has led to constitutions, social covenants, and procedures for negotiation that have survived for over two centuries, through one of the most trying periods of change in human history. Chapter ten asserts that modernity has much of value to offer to international relations; it explores the 16 intellectuals' suggested directions for the modernity of the nation-state.

I assert that there is much to be salvaged from old modernity in its methods for discovering rules about how the world works. Implied in first-wave modernity is agency for human beings: We are free and worthy of dignity and respect. German philosopher Jürgen Habermas has described this vision of modernity and its potential for valuing humans beings and solving problems as an "unfinished project" that has not yet been thoroughly mined for its potential for justice and empowerment. (Passerin d'Entrèves, 1996).

I likewise see the revitalization of modernity as the greatest hope for remaking and re-energizing the nation-state in a way that will create social justice. The first aspect of this revitalization may come from technophiles who understand finance, health care, or international relations well enough to ascertain when the players in these systems are *not* being modern; that is, when they are making an end-run around the rules intended to make such systems transparent and fair.

I am recommending a re-thinking of sovereignty and boundedness, and virtually a re-definition of unity. I recommend something like recommitment to modernity, like renewing marriage vows. Proceduralism, transparency and rationality are inexorable or guaranteed. Modernity depends on a complex infrastructure of an educated public, free and honest press, checks on governmental power, and basics like bureaucratic offices that function competently. This machinery and a simple commitment to the idea of modernity could be slowly but catastrophically eroded by forgetting the improvements in quotidian lives that modernity has made so far.

## Summary

If we draw a comparison between our own era and the late Renaissance, when a whole new entity, the nation-state, needed to be created, it might follow that a revitalized institution, some sort of globally functional, resilient postnational nation-state is necessary.

We are certainly not there yet. Monstrous devastations of humanity and the biosphere have been committed in the name of the nation-state and nationalism. I am not saying that the nation-state is intrinsically moral. We live with the legacy of neatly stacked skulls and the buried ashes from mass crematoriums. I am not saying that there is not now grinding deprivation exacerbated by the aftermath of colonialism and global economic entities (such as the I.M.F. and World Bank) that continue to privilege the interests of rich nations (and the multinational corporations headquartered in them) while further impoverishing poor nations. What is I am saying is that we cannot only think about the potential for social justice at the level of the community or the individual activist. We are in a 14 billion-legged sack race and if some of us stumble and fall, we all go down. In our interdependence, we need to revamp social structures on the largest scale. These social structures must begin to better address the exigencies of the global commons and our entangled fates. My suggestion is that the most promising macro social entity to retool is the nation-state, and that examination of public discourse at several levels bears this out.

The most prescient of public intellectuals have talked about how traditional dimensions of the nation-state need to evolve. Given both my findings in public discourse and special attention to the 16 public intellectuals upon who works I draw, I propose that that is precisely, *in the best case*, what will happen. It will dawn on us and our political and intellectual leaders that the rigidities of the 17th through 20th century nation-state will break the system if not softened while being made more precise. If this best scenario transpires, I believe that we will still call this flexible and sustainable entity the "nation-state."

# CHAPTER TWO. WHAT IS GOING ON WITH WORLD ORDER?

Predictions about world order. State-Centered versus Non State-Centered Views of World Order. The Endurance of the Nation-State. Non State-Centered Predictions: Ethnocultural Identity, Global Economy, Empire, or A Global Epoch? Whither from Here?

*

...And [the crew] lost radio contact when they went around the dark side of the moon and there was inevitably some suspense, and when they came back into radio contact they looked up and they snapped this picture and it became known as 'Earthrise.'

[This image] exploded into the consciousness of humankind. It led to dramatic changes and within 18 months the modern environmental movement had begun.

—Former Vice President Al Gore, *An Inconvenient Truth: A Global Warning*, (2006, DVD chapter 1: The River), describing the photograph of planet Earth taken on July 20, 1969 on the return trip of the Apollo 11 mission.

Our view of the nation-state and the viability of the planet itself have recently suffered bruising blows and dramatic reconfiguration: acts of non-state-on-state terrorism; the torrent of money, jobs, ideas, resources and threats across national boundaries; outbreaks of ethnically-driven genocide; new freedoms and capabilities; and the birth or reconfiguration of 31 nations since 1990. In two decades, eight new nations have sprung from former Yugoslavia and Czechoslovakia alone;

the former Soviet Union yielded another 15. Eritrea and East Timor seceded from Somalia and Indonesia, respectively, in 1993 and 2002. Namibia, the Republic of Palau, and Kosovo (a ninth new nation subsequent to the Bosnian conflicts) became independent in 1990, 1994, and 2008. In 1990, North and South Yemen united to form Yemen, and East and West Germany rejoined to form the Federal Republic of Germany. After the overthrow of General Mobutu Sese Seko in 1997, Zaire changed its name to the Democratic Republic of Congo. These 31 nation-state changes[4] since 1990 were exceeded only during the wave of African, Asian and Caribbean decolonization after 1941. Although the end of World War II (WWII) is certainly a monumental turning point in international dynamics, many of the more stunning shifts happened very recently. Moreover, the recent wave of nation-state reconfigurations took place in *fewer than half* of the forty years of nation-state births and changes following WWII.

Because of these sudden, numerous nation-state changes, as well as the challenges to the political nation-state from economic globalization, "What is going on with world order?" emerged as an important underlying question of this book. I've concluded in two analyses of public texts that the nation-state will prevail as the dominant macro social structure, and I believe that this is a good thing. However, the nation-state must embark on deep change or suffer slow death.

The years that followed the fall of the Berlin Wall were filled with more stunning implosions and openings—the August Putsch against Moscow, the dissolution of the Soviet Union by the end of 1991, and after that, waves of bloodshed in the Balkans.

---

[4] Not counted are the independence of the Marshalls Islands or Micronesia, nor the name changes of Western Samoa to Samoa, Republic of Fiji to the Republic of Fiji Islands after a military coup in 2006, or the Federal Islamic Republic of Comoros to the Union of Comoros Islands after its 18th military coup.

When the long Cold War between capitalism and the U.S.S.R. ended, public voices first predicted a convergent world in which there would finally be consensus that capitalism had bested fascism and communism. Together, the seeming resolutions[5] and unexpected upheavals shook the dominant secular institution—the nation-state—to its very roots.

Having pondered the puzzle of a non-state (al Qaeda) declaring war on a state (the U.S.) in 2001, and in response to the clash between Hezbollah and Israel during summer of 2006, I made my own prediction about an emergent social structure, the "virtual nation," driven by politicized ideology and not tied to any particular territory—propagating through other societies like a virus traveling through a living body. Other scholars and thinkers have predicted scenarios such as widespread chaos based on ethnic conflict, a new social order born of the desire to join the global economy, a return to a 21st century version of empire, and a new global epoch in which modern nation-states falter and fail. Former Vice President Al Gore articulated this last view in a popular context in the quotation at the beginning of this chapter. Martin Albrow explored this theory in a scholarly way in a book called *The Global Age* (1996).

## The World in Pieces

Another iconic event that sullied the image of a harmonious community of nation-states after the Cold War was the protest over the meeting of the W.T.O. in Seattle in December 1999. The vehemence and sheer diversity of dissent made pundits and politicians realize that globalization had an ominous penumbra—and that the global econom-

---

[5] I say "seeming resolutions" because the collapse of the Soviet Union and the end of the Cold War created as many problems as they solved.

ic playing field was perceived as neither flat nor level in providing opportunities for all comers. In fact, those who had long held power, including the players at the I.M.F. and the W.T.O., had continued to jealously guard their advantages, to the detriment—and wrath—of other players on the economic stage.

If the W.T.O. protests cast an unanticipated shadow over the end of the 20th century, the September 11 attacks of 2001 began the 21st century with another shock—that "super-empowered" groups and individuals could and would, Blofeld-style[6], engage nation-states in their cultural rage. Such groups include al Qaeda in its struggle for a return to Islamic preeminence, the Tamil Tigers, perpetrators of bombings in Mumbai, Madrid, London, Baghdad, and elsewhere., Hezbollah in its war with Israel in 2006, and Hamas and Fatah clashing over the West Bank, as well as violence from other non-states. These entities and conflicts all seemed to indicate the emergence of a changing social order, and possibly a new form of politico-military entity.

During the past two decades, Internet-enabled connections have made it possible for those traversing nation-state boundaries to hold onto national loyalties in an unprecedented way. This was yet another basic difference between the early post-Cold War period and previous surges in migration and globalization. Because of fast, low-cost, vivid communications, people could migrate to other countries for work but hold tightly, perhaps too tightly, to identities based in the countries of their birth. Service workers fueled globalization, but could not fully partake in the wealth or opportunities offered to citizens of the countries in which they worked. In effect, they were allowed to dry clean the professional attire of knowledge workers in global cities, but they were not invited to don that attire. Sociologist Saskia Sassen has ex-

---

[6] The villain created by Ian Fleming in the James Bond novels and films.

plored this dimension of globalization: how it widens rather than closes the gaps among some classes of workers. (Sassen, 1991, 1994, 1996a, 1996b, 1998, 2006).

## "We are seeing something new here..."

By early 2002, the Bush administration was preparing the American public for the invasion of Iraq. The Secretary of Defense at the time, Donald Rumsfeld, made statements in which it seemed he was groping to understand military conflict between a nation-state and a non-state.[7]

Like Rumsfeld, scholars and other authors had been scrambling to understand what was happening. They were responding to the events of the final decade of the 20th century and the beginning of the 21st, asking: What is going on with the nation-state? Is a "postnational" era dawning, in which the assumptions about world order will no longer revolve around the nation-state? If the nation-state is indeed breaking down, what will the emergent organization look like? Will the world decline into disconnected chaos like that seen in Europe after the fall of the Roman Empire? What will the nation-state become when it is not shaped by the tug-of-war between capitalism and communism?

All of these questions raise another one: What is the nation-state? Political scientists are among the few who actually use this hyphenated term. Regular folks say "nation," or "state," or "country."

Clifford Geertz asks, "What is a Country if it is not a Nation? What is a Culture if it is not a Consensus?" (2000, 218-30) He goes to the dictionary and employs his considerable understanding of different patterns among different peoples to find that "country" refers to the land, the landscape, the territory; that the Latin word for birth, "natio"

---

[7] Transcript, Press Conference with U.S. Secretary of Defense Donald Rumsfeld, April 25, 2002.

is tucked inside of "nation," implying the antiquated idea that a citizen is—first and foremost—born to his or her membership in a nation. Geertz then locates word roots for prestige and social placement in "estate" and "status" related to "state."

Thus we can see that that "nation-state" embodies a complex entanglement of ideas. The term means the government or "state" *plus* the "nation" it governs. The nation is made up of the people and the cultural patterns they supposedly share. The term "state" refers to the combination of government and the territory it supposedly controls.

I wrote "supposedly" twice in the last two sentences. Much that people have *supposed* about political order for three and a half centuries is now being called into question. The nation-state is one of the phenomena that holds the most sway over human life (along with human sexuality, religion, and money). Geertz wrote that the country, the nation, the nation-state are more than land, ethnicity, and monolithic agreement. However, we need to be aware of these older concepts at the heart of a renewed nation-state.

Though the term "nation-state" sounds pretty pompous to the ears of non-academics, the idea of the nation-state is still front and center in many public conversations. Tune in to breaking events, news analysis, or even satire, and the nation-state is suddenly everywhere. Delegates at the Republican National Convention in August 2008 held up signs and chanted, "Nation first!" With his tongue firmly in his cheek, Stephen Colbert greets the viewers of nearly every one of his shows by saying, "Nation...*nation*, [what I've been thinking about is...]"

And the pressures on and changes in the nation-state are at the forefront of prominent discourse. In a speech in April 2009 in a place that has sometimes been France and has sometimes been Germany, President Obama described a shrinking, interconnected world, and implied a re-thinking of the dominant secular institution. His speech either explicitly mentioned or alluded to all seven of what I have called the nation-state properties. My word count analysis of his speech reveals that the President of the United States is among world leaders who are beginning to discuss the necessary maturation of several of these nation-state functions, especially sovereignty and boundedness.[8]

In Strasbourg, a city that is a symbol of crossroads—crossroads of space, such as rivers, of culture, such as religion, and most importantly crossroads of social time, the President said "we've arrived at a moment where each nation and every citizen must choose at last how we respond to a world that has grown smaller and more connected than at any time in its existence." He reasserted this view in a speech at Cairo University in June 2009, alluding to the same properties of the dominant institution and saying to the assembly, "You more than anyone have the ability to re-imagine the world, then remake this world."

With these sorts of indicators in public discourse, particularly from world leaders, it's fair to ask: What is the nation-state supposed to do?[9] How is it supposed to function differently than it has for 350 years? What should its path be? The answers to these questions may seem abstract and arcane, but they will affect billions, since the nation-state is, at least for now, the highest level at which societies are recog-

---

[8] For additional analysis, see Redd, Adrienne. 2009/2010. Obama in Strasbourg: Crossroads of social time; sovereignty and boundedness April 9, 2010.
http://adrienneredd.wordpress.com/
[9] This question of what the nation-state is supposed to do is explored in chapter four. In asking what the nation-state is supposed to do, one opens the question of what *any* governmental entity is supposed to do. Municipalities and other local or regional governments sometimes attempt to preempt decision-making that might logically go to the nation-state government. Moving this locus of responsibility can be deeply problematic, as in the English decision to empower local governments to conduct surveillance. In other instances, local and regional governments try to move the responsibility to the Federal level, as in local bids for more money for public schools and other social services.

nized, at which policy is set, and at which social resources are allocated. Yes, there are international, even metanational projects, but they are still funded and legitimated by nation-states.

The nation-state is an abstraction but it has legitimacy, power, and a vast and pervasive influence because people say that it does. This point is connected to the third property of the nation-state—"attribution"—which I discuss in chapter four.

Soldiers are sent around the world, money is printed, and children receive two vegetables in subsidized school lunches (or only one) based on beliefs that ordinary people and politicians hold about the nation-state. Therefore, the ideas that intellectuals express and the collective beliefs people share do matter. What people convey in language becomes the material reality that is played out in everyday life and policy that affects everyday lives.

## State-Centered versus Non State-Centered Views of World Order

Political scientists and other writers in the public sphere didn't question the dominance of the nation-state until after WWII—and even then, not until the combined crises of industrial decline and U.S. involvement in the proxy conflict with the U.S.S.R. in Vietnam. A central concept of this chapter and this book is the difference between so-called "state-centered" and "non-state-centered" explanations of international affairs. Thomas P. M. Barnett (2004, 2005), a former professor of the U.S. Naval War College and one of the 16 public intellectuals, is a military strategist who advocates an empire-like "exportation of security" to quell violence as the impoverished and easily radicalized populations of third world nations join the globalized economy.

"State-centered" theorists hold that the nation-state will and should remain the dominant macro social structure. One group of writers making themselves heard after the end of the Cold War took the position that the nation-state is indispensable, saying that only the nation-state affords the possibility of representational democracy, constitutional protections, and the capacity for sheltered political dialogue that leads to social change. I call these writers, including academicians Paul, Ikenberry and Hall (2003), Lentner (2004), and to a lesser extent Hirst (2001), the "defenders of the nation-state." Despite assaults and changes, the nation-state is still seen as the enduring entity to turn to in time of trouble. It is with this view in mind that I propose the re-conceptualization of four nation-state properties.

## Four Families of Non State-Centered Views of World Order

Recent transfigurations and crises of the nation-state—the Asian and African independence movements, the fall of the Berlin Wall, the collapse of the Soviet Union, the breakup of Yugoslavia—led political scientists to put forth varying theories about what the central glue of world order might be in the future. When scientists think about something, they place a particular "object of analysis" at the center of their questions. Neurologists consider the nervous system; primatologists consider primates. Both might consider the nervous systems of primates, and they might or might not agree in their conclusions.

Similarly, political scientists can take the same object of analysis (ethnicity, the economy, etc.) and reach widely divergent conclusions. I have identifies the following four "non-state" explanations or predictions about the future of the global community:

- The "chaos" and "civilizational" theses, which I group together. These take sub-national identity based in **ethnicity, language or religion** as their object of analysis, and they predict irresolvable clashes between civilizations, or even total breakdown of the social order. The first quotation, heading the section on Ethnocultural Identity, is from the late U.S. Senator Daniel Patrick Moynihan (1992) and captures the ethnic chaos thesis. This group also includes the old Cold Warrior Chalmers Johnson—featured prominently in the documentary *Why We Fight*—(2005, dir. Eugene Jarecki) who has urgently warned *against* the degeneration of the American Republic into something like what Rome in its final days.

- Comparative harmony among people from diverse cultural backgrounds all striving to take part in the **global economy**. The thesis is that a desire—and new capabilities—to pursue material success will erase other divisive factors.

- A third body of writing centers on how social structures larger than nation-states (such as metanational projects or empire) might become the dominant organization to maintain order through a phase of intense change. Writings after 1990 emphasized a return to **empire** as the dominant social structure, with varying views on whether such a return is a good thing or not.

- **"Globalization theory"** seeks explanations for complex social effects while considering money or comparative material circumstances *and* cultural patterns, the aftermath of colonialism, and the increasing currents of people, money, resources and information across formerly impermeable national boundaries. British sociologist Martin Albrow (1996) theorized that the nation-state will cease to be the dominant macro social structure and,

27

instead believes that focus on the globe overall, in its fragility and finiteness, will become the dominant political paradigm.

There is also a small group of writers who speculate about the role of non-state actors. Arjun Appadurai (one of the 16 thinkers on whose work I draw) calls the \nation-state a "vertebral" social structure, and refers to non-state actors such as the Tamil separatists, Hamas, or al Qaeda as "cellular" social configurations. I discuss this more in chapter eight.

## Milk, or Terry Cloth, or Both, or Something Else?

A famous experiment in primatology was conducted in the 1950s. (Harlow, 1959). Baby rhesus monkeys were separated from their mothers and given a choice between wire "mothers" that held bottles of milk and terry cloth "mothers" that did not provide food but were comparatively soft and inviting. The babies visited bottle-holding mothers for food only and returned to the soft, fabric-covered surrogates to cuddle, as they would have with their living mothers.

The discovery of the affinity of the baby monkeys for cuddly "mothers," even when they did not provide food, is a metaphor for thinking about what humans need and what motivates them to coalesce into social patterns.

Predictions centering on money[10] correspond to the thesis that people are most motivated by milk. Similarly, we could argue that predictions emphasizing ethnocultural identity correspond to terry

---

[10] To say in this analysis that money (versus other emphases) is the central "glue" of society avoids many subtleties; comparative deprivation or material welfare is related to sociological theory that places work or social class at the center of social arrangements.

cloth, substituting for tactile reassurance—and even social connections for the baby monkeys. While Maslow's hierarchy of human needs seems to resolve this question of the basic motivations behind social organization, the differences in theory remain.

With milk representing economic motivations and terry cloth representing social connections, abstract institutions—whether nation-states (or something even bigger like empires or metanations)—are about rules for allocating "milk" or "terry cloth."

Such rules take the form of written and unwritten social contracts and procedures for executing such contracts. This gives us a focus on institutions that implement contracts and procedures. Max Weber was interested in the roles that institutions and bureaucracies would play in organizing society. He thought of bureaucracies not in a pejorative sense they have taken on, but rather as guardians of modernity and a rational process.

Though I've taken a page to consider social order as driven by *either* social yearnings *or* material needs, it's folly to try to explain human behavior in terms of one or the other. People are more complicated than monkeys; they are more unpredictable than what can be captured in recipes, or rule sets for resource allocation, or cultural affiliations. Globalization theory has developed to try to puzzle through the interactions between people being motivated by many factors. This chapter is a survey and categorization of predictions about what is going on with world order.

## Ethnocultural Identity

> 'The blood from the Balkans is seeping under Europe's door.'[11] In what had been Yugoslavia a Serb militiaman, part of a force besieging the Bosnian city of Gorazde, told of his village burnt, his brother-in-law dead. 'Serbs, naked and tortured.' He had responded in kind, 'I have cut the throats of three Turks so far, and I don't ever have nightmares.'[12]
>
> —Daniel Patrick Moynihan, *Pandaemonium: Ethnicity in International Politics,* (1993, 144).

Imagine traveling thought the wilds in the 12th century to get from one farm or feudal estate to another. Roads, except for those left by the Romans, were not smooth or well maintained. There were robbers and other human and animal predators. Even communication with well meaning strangers was not guaranteed. There were no emergency medical facilities. There were few guesthouses, no 24-hour markets— few food sources beyond what could be carried, killed or gathered. Water was not necessarily free of *e. coli* or cholera bacilli. If one suffered from intestinal distress, there were neither public toilets nor a place to wash up other than ground water.

Venturing outside the boundaries of one's village or town was dangerous, unhealthy, and unpleasant, which was why people didn't do it very often. After the fall of Rome, trade routes had shriveled, and people seldom went beyond the safe and familiar. This is why it was so remarkable, and important, to Europeans that Marco Polo and his

---

[11] Unsigned Editorial, "Silence Serbia's Big Guns," *The New York Times* (July 22, 1992): A18. See Opinion-Editorial Texts.

[12] Julijana Mojsilovic, "Serbs Tell a Bitter Story of War; Militiamen Besieging Town Say West Does Not Understand," *The Washington Post,* (August 4, 1992): All.

father and uncle *walked* from Venice through Mongolia, China, and the Asian subcontinent in the 14th century.

Proponents of the ethnic chaos thesis foresee a reversion to isolated islands of farms or burgs with treacherous pathless wastelands in between. James Kunstler (2005) even envisions this happening to suburbs of the U.S. as a result of escalating gasoline prices. In their view, ethnic strife will lead to a disconnected world. In fact, millions of square miles of the planet are like this now—cut off and dangerously disconnected from the rest of humanity outside tiny population concentrations.[13]

Theories focusing on ethnocultural identity as the central basis for elucidating events since 1990, generally depict a world first torn apart by differences in ethnicity, race, culture and religion, and then deglobalized.

The interconnected units of analysis in the "ethnic chaos" thesis, the "clash of civilizations" thesis, and warnings about "resurgent nationalism"[14] are cultural patterns that people assert are ancient—racial, ethnic, tribal and religious identity affiliation. Predictions of "chaos" and "anarchy" fueled by ethnocultural conflict date to the late 1970s and early 1980s. See, for example, Hedley Bull (1977), an early predictor of a breakdown of international stability, and Charles Foster (1980), who tracked separatism and unrest among ethnic minorities. After ethnoreligious political violence began in the former Yugoslavia, other scho-

---

[13] We can see this in horror movies—those cinematic catharses of isolation—which are are often set in rural areas, and less often are about urban monsters, though real life examples abound. The genre seems to be about disconnectedness—the disruption and atrophy of civilizing influences such as open lines of communication and safe travel.
[14] However, I try not to use the word "nationalism" to mean the building of new nations since it is almost always not a "nation-oriented" undertaking but an appropriation of ethnic group identity in distinctly non-national or sub-national grabs for power; the demagoguery of Slobodan Milošević is one of the best examples of this.

lars and thinkers like American journalist Robert Kaplan (1994), Moynihan (1993), futurists Toffler and Toffler (1993), and, later, academic Louise Gerdes (2006) predicted a widespread social breakdown unleashed by tribal competition.

The most famous work on cultural identity as the key adhesive or repellent social force is by Harvard professor Samuel Huntington (1993, 1996). In the summer of 1993, Dr. Huntington wrote an article for *Foreign Affairs* with a question mark after the hypothesis, "The Clash of Civilizations?" His article and later book (1996) postulated that there were seven major civilizations centered on China, India, Islam, the West, Africa, Japan and the Spanish-speaking world.[15] Huntington argued that the cultural ties within these seven civilizations would shape political alliances and that conflicts among them would be the basis of warfare and other tensions.

Interestingly, few writers have spent much energy debunking the chaos and civilization theses directly.[16] Cultural anthropologists

---

[15] Another background theorist is Bernard Lewis (1998, 2002, 2003), professor emeritus of Near Eastern Studies at Princeton. Lewis has examined the Quran and other primary texts in Arabic to better understand the macro social structures of the Islamic world—specifically focusing on the compatibilities and lack thereof between the modern Western world and Islam. His work is related to with chaos or civilizational theses. One of Lewis's main points is that "true" Islam *is concerned* with harmony, social justice, and an egalitarian society and that the radicalized "Islamist" meme is a gross perversion of the Quran. Lewis's three books in the Selected Bibliography and Cited References are quick and engaging reads, and shed much-needed light on both the insights and fallacies in Huntington.

[16] Yahya Sadowski (1998) examines empirical data on ethnically motivated clashes to dispute the ethnic chaos thesis. Sadowski points out that this is not the first time a scientific theory (in this case, chaos theory) has been shoehorned onto a postulation about social systems. (Chaos theory in science states in the simplest terms that some sufficiently complex systems are unpredictable; the "chaos" theory in political science is not a corollary but simply picks up on the attention-getting word, "chaos.") Sadowski argues that when the end of the Cold War created unforeseen upheaval, pre-

Besteman and Gusterson (2005, 9-11, 56-69) have noted the appeal of big, simple explanations that appear to make sense of our rapidly changing world and increasingly intertwined global destiny. The anthropologists are particularly damning of Robert Kaplan and Samuel Huntington, citing two fallacious assumptions that non-anthropologists sometimes make about traditional societies.

The first is the mistaken idea that a given society can be summed up, or "essentialized." Offensive examples might include: "The Chinese are inscrutable" or "Latino men are motivated by *machismo*." Neither Kaplan nor Huntington make generalizations quite this gross, but the over-generalization and racism of the ethnic chaos and civilizational theses intellectualize a deep-seated fear of "other," in Besteman and Gusterson's view.

The second is the assumption that "traditional" cultures are static. Besteman and Gusterson note that these cultures move, change, adapt, absorb influences, have internal divisions, and negotiate emergent norms just as we modern folks do. A common criticism of Huntington is to assert that Sino or Indo or Islamic culture is not a single, monolithic phenomenon. To see any given culture as unchanging is to fail to understand culture at a basic level.

## Whither from Here?

When I tell people that I am studying the changing perception of the nation-state, one of the first things that they ask is, "Well, if the nation-state is breaking down, what will happen next?" This is why I have outlined the major families of conjecture on this issue. The aca-

---

dictions such as Moynihan's and Kaplan's, bolstered with details from Huntington, anchored Americans and gave them a sense of direction—emphasizing the divisive role of ethnicity and culture.

demic and popular treatises that emphasize ethnocultural identity and connections are not optimistic, painting a picture of destruction and suffering.

Chaos is the "or else." The dire picture of a new dark age is the consequence threatened for not heeding the warnings of Kaplan, Huntington, Moynihan et al. Often, these warnings about chaos driven by ethnic differences or civilizational incompatibility serve as justifications for the use of force.

It would be foolish to try to sidestep ideology in a review of predictions about what is going on with world order, or in my own proposals for recommended evolution of the nation-state. I know from the community of my own colleagues that no social or political scientist picks up a new book without trying to pigeonhole it as "liberal" or "conservative," "socialist" or "libertarian." It's easy to make this mistake with the writers advancing ethnic or "civilizational" theories. Kaplan, Huntington and others get categorized as "law-and-order" guys or "hardliners," while the late Senator Moynihan and Michael Ignatieff (1993) can be categorized as "liberal" politicians who have advocated social intervention at both a national and international level. (Michael Ignatieff is one of the 16 public intellectuals whose selection I explain in chapter three). In my experience, oversimplifying the political affiliations of these leaders and intellectuals is a mistake. I find also that the extreme ends of the political spectrum wrap around and overlap with one another in their recommendations.

There is one more prediction related to the chaos thesis that I should mention. Weighing several scenarios for global organization, Hirst (2001) concludes that the current period of an open society may be ending, and that the liberal nation-state in an international community of states may be regarded in retrospect as having been a golden age (like the Golden Age of Greece or the Roman Republic before reversion to empire).

Hirst asserts that competition for planetary resources (clean water, soil, fuel, etc.) may drive a grisly deterioration of the international state system. Until very recently, few theorists advancing predictions about political order have considered that environmental competition may be the key factor in political relations in the future—specifically driving the scramble for water, land and energy that may look from the outside like ethnic genocide.

Evidence that not enough attention has been paid to this factor can be found in the greater emphasis on environmental sustainability and energy resilience in the Quadrennial Homeland Security Review (QHSR) released by the U.S. Department of Homeland Security February 1, 2010. It's remarkable how long it's taken security experts to realize that natural resources may be the thing most worth fighting for in centuries to come. Hirst (2001) and Robb (2007), and, his earlier thesis quoted below about the leveling playing field of the global economy, Friedman (2008) are among the few who have linked political assessment with cognizance of environmental degradation.

## Global Economy

Following the pioneering release of the Apple II home computer by Steve Jobs and Steve Wozniak in 1977, the first IBM PC (personal computer) hit the markets in 1981. The first version of the Windows operating system launched in 1985, and the breakthrough [graphical user interface, modeled after Apple's Macintosh] that made IBM PCs much more user-friendly—Windows 3.0—shipped on May 22, 1990, only six months after the [Berlin] wall went down. While the fall of the wall eliminated a physical and geopolitical barrier—one that held back information, stood in the way of shared standards, and kept us from having a view of the world as a single unified community—the rise of the Windows-enabled PC ... eliminated another hugely important barrier....

—Thomas Friedman, *The World is Flat: A Brief History of the 21st Century* (2005/2006, 55-56)

Emphasis on the global economy as the phenomenon most likely to shape world order includes two books and hundreds of articles by *New York Times* columnist Thomas Friedman (another of the 16). Friedman proposed in *The Lexus and the Olive Tree* (1999/2000) that the world would be politically split between a desire to participate in the global economy, symbolized by the Lexus, and the desire to retain identity and traditions, symbolized by the olive tree. He expanded further on this, exploring ten trends—that he claimed were converging—or "flattening" or leveling the opportunity to improve one's economic lot. These range from the fall of the Soviet Union to personal computing to the Internet to convergence of technological capabilities (such as printing your own flight boarding pass at home) that place more responsibility (and risk) on the individual.

Cheerleaders for the "flattening" capacity of globalization also include investment expert George Gilder (2000), MIT technologist William Knoke (1996), futurists John Naisbitt (1982, 1994) and Alvin Toffler (1995), and academic Richard Rosecrance (1996, 2000). Rosecrance first postulated in an article entitled "The Rise of the Virtual State" (and later in a book of the same name) that nation-states would become "virtual."

That is, Rosecrance posited, nation-states would begin to advocate for opportunities on behalf of the multinational corporations based in their territory.

Gilder, Knoke and Toffler heralded the information-based economy as a bellwether of prosperity and peace in the political world. With impressive accuracy, Naisbitt (1982) predicted major global shifts based on his tracking of word-prevalence in newspapers in the 1970s and early 1980s. These shifts included streamlining production methods for physical products, "mass customization" of speedily updated and electronically-delivered information products, just-in-time production, and worldwide interdependence—a new dynamic within which small number of players such as innovators (and terrorists) could have an impact on thousands, even millions of people.

Following a path similar to Rosecrance's and Naisbitt's is the sweeping work of political science by Philip Bobbitt, a law professor at the University of Texas at Austin, entitled *The Shield of Achilles*. Bobbitt (2002, 346-347) traces the history of the state from "princely state" to "kingly state" to "territorial state" to "state-nation" to "nation-state," culminating in what he calls the "market-state." John Robb, a retired U.S. Air Force officer, updates, refines and focuses this prediction further in a 2007 paper entitled, "Nation-states, market-states, and virtual-states." Robb predicts that the market-state will abandon the traditional responsibility of providing material well-being for its citizens and will afford them global economic *opportunity* instead. In chapters seven and eleven I discuss the traditional responsibilities expected of the nation-state, including maintenance of a social safety net—which Bobbitt, Rosecrance, and anthropologist and social geographer David Harvey (1989, 2003), predict will be abandoned—in chapters seven and eleven.

Finally, no discussion of the social effects of the global economy is complete without mentioning the work of Moises Naím (2005), a Venezuelan author and journalist who has been the editor-in-chief of *Foreign Policy* magazine since 1996; Joseph Stiglitz (2003); and George Soros (2000, 2002), a financier who has turned his attention to understanding the injustices perpetrated by the global economy. All three assert that the rules of a supposedly "flat" global economy are either flouted by criminals or unfairly applied by the very authorities who are charged with upholding them. In the view of Naím, Stiglitz and Soros, more transparent rules are necessary to prevent exploitation via selective rule enforcement—and resultant protest, mutiny, and instability. These writers caution that *nobody* will be able to reap the harvest of a "flattened world" if angry peasants burn the crops because of their rage over all the ways in which the global economy exploits them and if they then frame that exploitation as ethnocultural competition. History has seen wildfire riots in Chicago and Cincinnati in which people victimized by racial segregation and poverty destroyed what little they had rather than try to get onto the not-yet-flat-enough playing field of exurban job opportunities.

## Warnings About, and Recommendations of Return to, Empire

> "[R]ule sets" [are a] collection of rules that delineate how some activity normally unfolds. ...These rules tell you how to keep score in the game, what constitutes unfair play, and how everyone is supposed to behave when they're on the field or court. ...[Y]ou can't start playing baseball by football rules or vice versa. So playing by the appropriate rule set is how we keep any game from collapsing into chaos. It's why we have referees and umpires; they enforce the rules so everyone gets roughly the same chance to succeed.
>
> —Thomas P.M. Barnett,• *The Pentagon's New Map* (2004, 9-10)

Most thinkers from both inside and outside the ivory tower of academia focus on empire as the manifestation of supranational social structure that is most worthy of debate and analysis. In early 2003, Thomas P.M. Barnett, a professor of warfare analysis, published an article in *Esquire* that used a geographical analysis of the globe's most troubled places to categorize some nation-states as the "disconnected gap," (comprised of the Middle East, much of Africa, and other poor and unstable countries), in contrast to the "operating core," (comprised of the U.S., U.K., Europe, China and others that play by "the rules"). Barnett recommended "exporting security" to the "dangerously disconnected" regions to bring them up to speed with the rest of the globalizing world and help make them more politically stable.

Barnett's work bears some similarity to that of Kaplan (1994, 2005) and Hardt and Negri (2004), who assert that something like imperial control is necessary to protect against terrorism and calm the troubled waters of societies changing at different rates.

Chalmers Johnson (2000, 2004, 2006) is one of the main voices arguing *against* a return to empire as the dominant social structure. Johnson says that using arbitrary military force to protect narrow nation-state interests will lead to bankruptcy (in terms of both ideas and finances) and, ultimately, to delegitimation of the (American) nation-state. Having spent his career working against the Soviet Union, Johnson came to the belief that American military force had become over-extended, covert, arbitrary, and too expensive.

Robb (2007) is a critic of Barnett (2004) and other advocates for a return to empire, questioning Barnett's assumption that centralized control of foreign locales or state-building projects is even possible, let alone morally justifiable. Barnett would claim that the stabilization he calls for in two books (2004, 2005) will happen through global rule but local control. Robb's concern about this is how the path of local control can be navigated so that pressured governments in "gap" countries don't collapse but neither that it become necessary for outside forces to step in. Nowhere is this concern more urgently played out than in Afghanistan and Pakistan.

## A Global Epoch?

> ... [T]he nation-state loses control of the forces it previously contained. The ensuing fragmentation is the result, even as nation-state societies cover the earth's surface. It is this penalty of success, which needs most to be understood. Individuals can understand it in terms of personal projects as the anti-climax, the let down, the feeling of

nothing to look forward to, the loss of a dream.

—Martin Albrow, The Global Age: State and Society beyond Modernity (2004, 64-65)

The word "globalization" has been the rallying cry expressing an anguished sense that something is very different in the past quarter century—and possibly very wrong. Globalization theory (which includes Martin Albrow's globality thesis) explores the impact of material conditions ("milk"), cultural patterns ("terry cloth") and increasing global interdependence so as to offer explanations of current and future planetary relations. The approach of globalization theorists is to take many factors into account as national borders are dissolving, transactions and communication are accelerating, resources are in greater supply in the wealthy West than in the formerly colonized rest of the world, and the rules for attaining such identity, comfort, or connectedness appear incompatible from one macroregion to the next.

## The Endurance of the Nation-State

My doctoral research revealed that, despite the many predictions to the contrary, it was the nation-state that endured in the minds of the writers whose letters and editorials I read. Even in responding to bloodshed and disorder, writers called upon the nation-state, both in general and in particular. They used metaphors of federally organized decision-making (central government that nonetheless defers to regional governments such as those of states and provinces). Even non-Americans referred to the first U.S. Continental Congress when they talked about international conflicts from 1946 through 2008.

The aim of the research was to search for perceptions of a postnational world. I classified popular and scholarly (mostly books) into four families of *non-state*-centered predictions: ethnocultural identity, empire, upheavals of globalization, and the (optimistically inter-

40

preted) desire to participate in the global economy. The purpose of this was to be able to recognize "postnational" perceptions in the newspaper texts when I came across them. Under the heading, Objects of Analysis, chapter six further discusses how the actual newspaper text corresponded to the four families of predictions about changing world order.

After the fall of the U.S.S.R., some thinkers suggested that macro social structures (other than empires) larger than nation-states might develop to coordinate political affairs for hundreds of millions of people across continents or even hemispheres. The most important example of this came from Robert Cooper (2003), whose vision for cooperation among nation-states through a metanational structure, the E.U., has significantly shaped this project. The other substantive discussion is from his colleague and superior at the E.U., Javier Solana (2004). The rising E.U. represents a hybrid organization that will rely on the nation-state as a continuing and important structure and will bridge communications, cooperation, and now security issues through a metanational structure. It will be important to see whether public thinkers believe that the E.U. model can address the problems currently the responsibility of the nation-state.

# CHAPTER THREE. A CASTLE BUILT OF WORDS

What is "public discourse"? Why these 16 leaders and public intellectuals? How their speeches and writing illuminate re-conceptualizations of nation-state properties.

*

I adopt the term imaginary ... because my focus is on the way ordinary people 'imagine' their social surroundings, and this is often expressed in theoretical terms, but it is carried in images, stories, and legends. It is also the case that ... theory is often the possession of a small minority, whereas what is interesting in the social imaginary is that it is shared by large groups of people, if not the whole society.

—Charles Taylor, *Modern Social Imaginaries* (2004, 23)

I recently asked Pennsylvania State Senator Daylin Leach what he estimated the chances were of passing his recently introduced bill for gay marriage in the Keystone State. He replied, "Short-term? Zero. Long-term? It's inevitable. In 20 years we will look back and think about objections to gay marriage the way we currently regard segregation. We will be astonished and ashamed that anybody ever thought that way."

Political change—such as Senator Leach's gay marriage bill, or civil rights for African Americans, or immigration reform, or the sort of rarified rethinking of the nation-state that I advocate—happens because of political talk.

This chapter defines public discourse and explains the selection criteria for the 16 leaders and public intellectuals. The purpose of examining their work is to show how their writings support rethinking four properties of the nation-state.

## What is "Public Discourse"?

Discourse is talk. Public discourse consists of ideas accessible to more than one person and conveyed in language. It can take the form of speech or writing. It is public because it is repeated, reinforced, or refuted by other people who don't personally know the person who first stated the idea. This includes stand-up comedy, classroom lectures, letters to the editor, blogs, treatises, and popular books. For discourse to be public or political, it must concern power—who makes the rules, who sets or defines the norms. In each of the forms of discourse I mention above, speakers point to sources of power and question them or construct formative assertions.

In my choice of language here I want to convey to the reader that, although I have chosen texts from 16 erudite minds, I also have been listening carefully to public discourse on the nation-state, control, boundaries, ethnic and other identity, and the contested issues of progress and modernity in humor, satire, common speech, and the speeches of public officials. I assert that what we say—and the words we use—light the way to where we are going, and that we have some influence over that direction if we listen to, understand the subtext of, and even try to shape public talk.

Comedy and drama, for example, can be deeply normative. Drama may be used to exaggerate the morally repugnant in order to convey a need for change. Consider the recent BBC miniseries[17] in which aliens

---

[17] Lyn Euros, director, *Torchwood: Children of Earth*, BBC, July 20-24, 2009.

seeking to abduct ten percent of the world's children point out to British diplomats that three children die from neglect every second, while Earth's leaders merely adjust to this fact without trying to change it. This colorful media artifact makes a compelling moral observation. Where is the moral outrage we should feel at the number of casualties of poverty and the gap between the rich and the poor?

Consider also the groundbreaking ways that comedians such as Richard Pryor, Chris Rock, and Dave Chappelle have forced mainstream audiences to reconsider American race relations. Dave Chappelle shone a blistering light on the social construction of race in his famous sketch on the Black White Supremacist.[18] We are black or white because we believe we are. We are Americans or Romanians or Eritreans because we collectively agree that we are. We build a castle of the nation-state with words that convey our imagining, and then we live in it together. The "castle" as a social construction doesn't physically exist, but it does operationally exist. Monetary exchange, family, and legality are shared beliefs that people inhabit and that affect their lives every day.

Public discourse is public because it evokes a response. Each of the 16 public figures I've selected has made thoughtful assertions that have affected public and international policy.

The German sociologist Jürgen Habermas (1996) describes the role of language used by lawyers and diplomats to create the procedural-constitutional "unity" of a nation-state, while writers, historians, and journalists construct the imagined cultural unity of the nation-state.

---

[18] Dave Chappelle, *Clayton Bigsby, the Black White Supremacist*, Comedy Central. Accessed July 24, 2009.
http://thetravisty.com/Chappelles_Show/wmv/Black_White_Supremacist.htm

Discourse also includes the silence that frames and punctuates words. The dearth of jokes about the events of September 11, 2001 was telling.[19] The storied analyst of mass media, Marshall McLuhan (1964), theorized that any given medium is hot or cold. I prefer to think about messages being positioned on a spectrum between hot (earnest, straightforward) and cold (ironic, detached, ridiculous). The events that Tuesday were far too hot for anything as detached as jokes. Compare the silence after 9/11 to the jokes after the destruction of the Challenger Shuttle in 1986. Just a few days after the Challenger disaster, we heard "What was the last thing said on the Challenger? 'What happens if I push *this* button...?'"

There was little language that addressed the pain of September 11, but public discourse often concerns the contested, the contentious, and the painful. One cannot write in the public sphere without having others disagree. Speech is intended to produce a response. The more important the topic, the greater the response.

## Six Diplomats, Six Scholars and Four Authors— Why these 16?

Short profiles of each of the 16 public intellectuals that I have chosen to reference appear below. In books, essays, editorials, and other statements, each of the 16 has at various points imagined the properties of the nation-state in a post-Westphalian way. In the belief that objectivity is a chimera, I offer some background on my perception of

---

[19] In a glimpse into the process of making humor about pain, *The Onion* editor Rob Siegel and writer Todd Hanson told Terry Gross three weeks after the attacks that they had rejected the joke headline "America stronger than ever, say Quadragon officials". Rob Seigel and Todd Hanson, interview by Terry Gross, *Fresh Air*, NPR, October 4, 2001.

the personhood and ideology of the authors so the reader will be able to place them.

*Six Diplomats:*

- George Shultz, born 1920 in New York, New York. Economist and U.S. Secretary of State (1982-1989). He continues to lecture and is a distinguished fellow at Stanford University's Hoover Institution.

- Zbigniew Brzezinski, born 1928 in Warsaw, Poland; U.S. National Security Advisor (1977–1981).

- Kofi Annan, born 1938 in Kumasi, Ghana; U.N. General Secretary (1997-2006). He earned an M.S. from MIT's Sloan School of Management.

- Michael Ignatieff, born 1947 in Toronto, Canada; majority leader of the opposition Liberal Party of Canada, Canadian Parliament (2008-present).

- Robert Cooper, born 1947 in Brentwood, Essex, U.K.; Director-General for External and Politico-Military Affairs, General Secretariat of the Council of the E.U. (2002-present). He holds an M.S. in International Relations from Oxford's Worcester College.

- Javier Solana, born 1948 in Madrid, Spain; Secretary General of NATO (1995-1999), E.U. High Representative for the Common Foreign and Security Policy (1999-2009).

Former Secretary of State George Shultz is the oldest of this group of statesmen, scholars and authors, all of whom are alive as of this writing. He continues to contributes opinion pieces to periodicals and to lecture on American foreign policy. Similarly, former National Security Advisor Brzezinski has written about international politics for more than 45 years.

From the work of Former U.N. Secretary General Annan, I drew on four editorial texts, three addresses, a chapter in a book, and his account of the genocide in Rwanda.

Canadian opposition party leader Michael Ignatieff is the most prolific writer among this group of six politicians. His thinking constitutes a bridge between political advocacy and scholarship. I considered his conceptualization and reconceptualization of sovereignty, nation-state boundedness, national unity and modernity in six books, four texts produced for the public sphere (including the one in which he reverses his opinion on whether the United States should have invaded Iraq in 2003), and a chapter on human rights and when states should intervene in other states experiencing humanitarian crises. Ignatieff is central because of his liminal place between theory and practice. In his public reversal on the invasion of Iraq, he says, "In political life, false ideas can ruin the lives of millions and useless ones can waste precious resources. An intellectual's responsibility for his ideas is to follow their consequences wherever they may lead. A politician's responsibility is to master those consequences and prevent them from doing harm." The most recent Ignatieff text listed here (2007) had the deepest impact on this book because in it Ignatieff tries to understand the mistake of advocating more broadly for intervention, that is, of violating sovereignty in times of crisis. I believe that "Human Rights, Power and the State" begins a new chapter for an already formidable thinker—a chapter on how to strike the balance between ideals and humane practice.

Beginning, "[O]ur language has not caught up with modernity...." the final passage of Ignatieff's book on social problems, *The Needs of Strangers* (1984, p. 141) had a tremendous impact as I contemplated modernity versus social cohesion, including a sense of a belonging in a dizzyingly mobile society.

For over ten years, Director-General Cooper has been working and re-working his ideas about how the underlying principles of the international community have changed since the end of the Cold War. Cooper's contribution to the idea of a reconceptualized nation-state is *The Breaking of Nations* (2003c), portions of which appear in earlier essays and a pre-September 11 version of the book. I also considered four of his public texts (2003a, 2003b, 2006a and 2006b), as well as two public statements. Robert Cooper reports to Javier Solana, who announced as this book was being written that he would complete his term and leave office in October 2009.

High Representative Solana gave a key speech in 1998 and has since written about how his positions and policies have changed, first as head of NATO and then working on policy for the E.U.

Each of the six diplomats I have chosen has been reviled at one time or another: Former Secretary of State George Shultz for molding and then defending a preemptive military policy, Zbigniew Brzezinski for isolating and pressuring U.S.S.R. and Soviet satellites, Kofi Annan for not doing more to stop genocide in Rwanda, Michael Ignatieff for not having lived his entire life in Canada before entering politics there and for changing his mind about whether the U.S. should attack Iraq, Robert Cooper for supporting and advising British Prime Minister Tony Blair in an interventionist foreign policy, and Javier Solana for opposing Spain's entry into NATO before taking its helm a mere 13 years later.

*Six Scholars:*
- Zygmunt Bauman, born 1925 in Poznań, Poland, professor emeritus of sociology at the University of Leeds.

- Jürgen Habermas, born 1929 in Düsseldorf, Germany; philosopher and sociologist; professor emeritus of Sociology at the University of Frankfurt.

- Charles Taylor, born 1931 in Montreal, Quebec, Canada; philosophy professor emeritus at McGill University.

- Abdullahi Ahmed An-Na'im, born 1950 in Khartoum, Sudan, professor of human rights and Islamic law at Emory University.

- Arjun Appadurai, born 1949 in (formerly) Bombay, India, cultural anthropologist, co-founder of the journal *Public Culture*; Senior Advisor for Global Initiatives at The New School.

- Joseph Stiglitz, born 1943 in Gary, Indiana. Nobel Laureate in economics; senior vice president and chief economist of the World Bank (1997-2000).

Zygmunt Bauman is widely considered the foremost scholar of globalization and the toll it takes on community and the quality of human life. An avowed communist, Bauman is the originator of the concept of "liquid modernity"—profit-driven, short-term maximization of utility that abandons social covenants and structures. This is an idea upon which Pepe Escobar (another of the 16, introduced below) builds in *Globalistan* (2006), exploring the metaphor of liquid (not solid or reliable) modernity, but also liquid gold—petroleum—which ends up shaping policy and international relations. Of Bauman's more than 60 books, I concentrated on five that appear in the bibliography as sources of his ideas on the changes taking place for sovereignty, nation-state boundedness, and modernity. The implication of the metaphor of liquid modernity used by both of these writers is that while we need to make boundaries "softer" and more pliable, we need to solidify modernity, in the sense of its becoming more reliable and less arbitrary.

Jürgen Habermas is another candidate for the title of greatest living philosopher and sociologist. He has contributed seminal writing about "public sphere," the idea of a shared forum—whether physical or virtual—where people engage in the exchange and refinement of ideas, many of which can be potently formative for society as a whole. From his dozens of major works, I list nine books in the bibliography. I have particularly emphasized the essay "The European Nation-state—Its Achievements and Its Limits" (1996), the essays in *The Postnational Constellation* (2003), and those in *Philosophy in a Time of Terror* (2004).

All of the 16, with the exception of Jürgen Habermas, wrote their speeches and texts in English. This emphasis on English was also true of the selection of newspaper texts for the research for the purpose of making linguistic comparison easier.

Charles Taylor is a Canadian philosopher who has considered how the very different desires, needs, and identities of groups under the aegis of a procedural nation-state can be met with justice and respect. I give the most attention by far to Taylor's book length essay, *Multiculturalism* (1994), but also consider three more of his books in the Bibliography in connection with works on identity by Bauman, Habermas, and Appadurai.

Abdullahi Ahmed An-Na'im has argued for the secular state as a way to preserve the integrity of religious practice. I have drawn upon his chapter and conclusion in a book he edited, *Human Rights in Cross-Cultural Perspectives* (1992), as well as his recent book, *Islam and the Secular State: Negotiating the Future of Shari'a* (2008).

Cultural anthropologist Arjun Appadurai has worked with the idea of the social imaginary, a concept also explored by Taylor and classically advanced by Benedict Anderson (1983/2006) with regard to the nation-state. Appadurai's early work (1996) on globalization was groundbreaking in trying to understand how new economic capabilities interact with new informational and social capabilities. The book he edited, *Globalization* (2001), drew on texts first published in *Public*

*Culture*, the journal that Appadurai founded with his wife, Carol Breckenridge. I have also examined some of Appadurai's papers in *Public Culture* and elsewhere. (Charles Taylor has also been a contributor to *Public Culture*.) However, I devote most of my attention to *Fear of Small Numbers* (2006), in which Appadurai examines the old idea of ethnic unity of the nation-state. For all of the writers, and particularly for the scholars, I drew most heavily on works written after September 11, 2001.

Joseph Stiglitz is neither a social scientist nor a philosopher. He is a Nobel Prize winning economist who served as a cabinet level advisor in the Clinton administration and went on to work as the chief economist at the World Bank. He opened my eyes to the ways in which the economic behemoths tout their allegiance to free markets while carefully protecting their own and forcing open the markets of poorer countries. Stiglitz rounds out the representation of metanational perspectives—along with Kofi Annan of the U.N., Javier Solana from NATO and the E.U., and Robert Cooper from the E.U.

An economist, Joseph Stiglitz writes as a social scientist while elucidating why the macro social structures set up to ameliorate global material inequality are not attaining that goal as well as they might. Adjacent to Stiglitz is Zygmunt Bauman, who likewise decries the social injustices of globalization. Bauman calls himself a "committed communist."[20] That Stiglitz, a former advisor to a mainstream American president appears to the "left" of Bauman in this illustration shows that left and right are really not useful concepts in trying to sort out predictions about the trajectory of international relations.

---

[20] Aida Edemariam, "Professor with a past," *The Guardian*, (April 28, 2007). Accessed April 3, 2009
www.guardian.co.uk/books/2007/apr/28/academicexperts.highereducation

| Stiglitz | Bauman | Taylor | Appadurai | An-Na'im | Habermas |
|---|---|---|---|---|---|
| Finance-Material inequality | Material inequality-Community | Social inequality-Community | Culture-Community | Law-Culture | Social structures constructed through reasoned and productive communication |

Charles Taylor is concerned with one very specific dimension of globalization—the heterogeneity of communities and macrocommunities (such as the nation-state) that aim to place people from very different linguistic, religious, and ethnic backgrounds under one universalist set of rules. As a Canadian, he is keenly aware that his homeland is perhaps one state, but at least three nations—Anglophones and Francophones with colonialist origins, and the First Nation of indigenous people.

Appadurai raises concerns similar to Taylor, but from a very different perspective, since he was born in Bombay and is a cultural anthropologist rather than a philosopher. Appadurai is multidisciplinary and more ethnographic in his approach.

An-Na'im, like Appadurai, has been transplanted from a place, Sudan, still struggling with which portions of modernity to adopt and which to reject. An-Na'im is a legal scholar, so his primary subject is the law, but his focus is on equitable application of laws across diverse cultural groups. Finally, the concerns of Habermas are rationality and language and the politically and legally relevant actions that spring from them.

*Four Journalists/Authors:*

- Thomas Friedman, born 1953 in St. Louis Park, Minnesota. Three-time Pulitzer Prize-winning columnist for *The New York Times*. He earned a masters of philosophy in Middle Eastern Studies from Oxford.

- Pepe Escobar, born 1954 in Brazil and based in Sao Paulo, Brazil; columnist for *Asia Times Online* and analyst for The Real News Network. An old-fashioned, peripatetic and multilingual investigative reporter for the *Asia Times* who has researched international events on every inhabited continent.

- Thomas P.M. Barnett, born 1962 in Chilton, Wisconsin. Military strategist, author, lecturer, and blogger.

- Fareed Zakaria, born 1964 in Mumbai, India. Journalist for *Time*, author, and television host specializing in international relations.

One can embrace or reject Thomas Friedman and his work, but— either way—it is difficult to be indifferent to him. Friedman's point of view might be described as "readiness for globalization." I examined three of his books and hundreds of his *New York Times* editorials, focusing on the portions of his work that reflected his conception of sovereignty, boundedness, nation-state unity, and modernity.

Brazilian columnist Pepe Escobar is the author of "Get Osama! Now! Or else." published by *Asia Times Online* two weeks before the terrorist attacks of September 11, 2001. He is an analyst for The Real News Network and has written on the economic interests motivating Western imperialism (particularly that of the U.S.). I principally examined his book *Globalistan: How the Globalized World is Dissolving into Liquid War* (2006), along with a number of his editorial texts. Friedman and Zakaria are part of "old media" or "big media," while Escobar contributes to new news media.

Thomas P.M. Barnett has a Ph.D. from Harvard (he was a student of Samuel Huntington) and was a professor at the Naval War College until the unexpected success of his first book, *The Pentagon's New Map* (2004), made him unwelcome there. Like Friedman, he is committed to the complex enterprise of the modern global economy. He characterizes the world as divided between an economically integrated "core" and a resistant "gap." He advocates an American-run state-building program around the world to build connectedness and promote globalization, and is more willing than most of the other thinkers to contemplate the use of force to forward this project. Unlike any of the other thinkers, he has a "day job" in the industrial sector, working as a "rainmaker" for U.S. government contractor Enterra Solutions LLC.

Finally, I drew on a number of Fareed Zakaria's editorial texts in *Time*, as well as two of his books: (1) *The Future of Freedom* (2003), in which Zakaria points out that majoritarian democracy does not intrinsically protect minorities in a diverse society; and (2) *The Post-American World* (2008), an examination of how the world beyond America's borders is rising in prosperity and influence.

| Escobar | Friedman | Zakaria | Barnett |
|---|---|---|---|
| Fundamental critique of established order | Outrage at Western transgressions | Protection of minorities | Willing to intervene on behalf of "new world order" |

The authors/journalists may also be displayed on an ideological continuum. Pepe Escobar is the most committed to what we might call critical theory, questioning power arrangements, inequalities, and secret agendas of Great Powers as they push around other countries, particularly in Southeast Asia and the Middle East. Though criticized by academics (Besteman and Gusterson, 2005) for his cheerful assertions that developing countries simply need to get on the same page as the first world in terms of work ethic and participation in the global economy, Thomas Friedman (2005) has certainly expressed moral outrage at American transgressions. Fareed Zakaria is sometimes described as a libertarian. His work reveals a passionate commitment to the protection of minority and marginalized people. Thomas Barnett, not a journalist but an author, public speaker, and blogger, is ready to contemplate military intervention in and control of the world's most unstable regions, and thus can be viewed as the most hawkish on the "intervention scale" of ideas advanced by these four writers.

*Summary:*

In selecting these thinkers, I strove to maximize diversity along a number of dimensions. Diplomats, scholars, and authors are all engaged in the world, but in very different ways.

I didn't employ any quota system of people of color or citizens of the developing world versus wealthy countries on this very short list. These men are idea-people whose work I encountered in trying to make sense of public perception about the direction of political order. So, sadly there are no women on this list. One might construct the argument that women have entered the political area recently enough that they have not yet been able to contribute the decades of both prominence and publishing of their ideas. By and large, men have been able to because, largely, someone else is working that second shift of coordinating domestic life, doing the dishes, connecting with family, etc.

Acknowledging this lack, the small group of 16 thinkers is astonishingly representative of the beliefs and colors of the world. The group includes two Canadians, an Englishman educated in Kenya, two Poles (counting Brzezinski by virtue of his dual citizenship), a Spaniard, a German, and a Brazilian. Notably missing is a statesman from China.

An-Na'im, Brzezinski, Appadurai and Zakaria are naturalized American citizens born in Sudan, Poland and Bombay/Mumbai, India, respectively. Arjun Appadurai is of Tamil ancestry on his mother's side and grew up speaking Tamil, Gujarati, Marathi, and Hindi. There are four other Americans, which does not reflect the demographics of the globe, but does reflect both the control of 59 percent of the world's resources by six percent of its population, as well as the influence of the United States on the planetary stage.

There are practicing Catholics, at least one Muslim, a Hindu by family origin, Jews by family origin, cultural Protestants, and non-believers. Michael Ignatieff identifies himself as a Russian Orthodox. This range of places of birth, race, belief structure, native language and other ways the 16 might be categorized is all the more remarkable when the resonance of their thoughts about the nation-state is considered.

# CHAPTER FOUR. SEVEN PROPERTIES OF THE NATION-STATE

Conceptualization of the nation-state in Enlightenment thought. Nation-State properties from 1946-1991. State-centered theorization 1991 to the present. Postnational prognostications.

\*

Every era asks, 'What is the State supposed to be doing?' The answer to this question provides us with an indication of the grounds of the State's legitimacy, for only when we know the purpose of the State can we say whether it is succeeding.

—Philip Bobbitt, *The Shield of Achilles* (2002, 177).

In the first chapter, I explained that the treaties that ended thirty years of war between Catholics and Protestants in Germany between 1618 and 1648 recognized the various aggrieved parties in the conflict as legal *persons*[21] on equal footing, in terms of the agreements and compensations prescribed. Historians refer to these treaties collectively as the Peace of Westphalia and political scientists point to them as a starting point for what is now the dominant political institution in the world. In this chapter, I identify and explain seven functions of this

---

[21] This idea of organization treated as legal persons is related but not identical to the status of corporations whose free of speech rights as persons was expanded in the catastrophic Supreme Court decision of January 22, 2010: Citizens United v. Federal Election Commission, No. 08-205.

still-most-powerful institution, the nation-state. Specifically, I discuss the following:

1. Sovereignty
2. Nation-state boundedness
3. Legitimacy and attribution
4. Protection and provision of social welfare
5. Lawfulness
6. "Unity"
7. Modernity

Although the issue of the expected properties of the nation-state seems lofty and abstract, this institution matters because it allocates real resources to real human beings—people may live or die based on whether they are protected—or their well-being fostered during times of disaster or misfortune.

These seven expected properties have their origins in the establishment of the equal legal footing of the entities (duchies, kingdoms, independent city-states) listed in the Peace of Westphalia. The nation-state's (perceived) prerogative to be self-directed and not interfered with by other political entities have evolved from the starting point of the treaties.

The seven nation-state properties can be categorized into three levels: First, sovereignty, boundedness, and attribution. These three are necessary for the nation-state to function as it was first conceptualized; therefore they are *operational* properties of the nation-state. Protection of (and provision for) and law and order can be grouped second. These properties are the most tangible services that citizens receive in return for relinquishing *some* freedoms; therefore, these are *reciprocal* properties of the nation-state—what the nation-state does for people in return for their transferring some of their self-determination to the government. Even before the codification of the modern nation-state,

Thomas Hobbes, Max Weber and other foundational writers theorized about citizens trading some of their liberties for protection by the state.

Today, in simplest terms, the extent of this trade-off constitutes the division between American liberals and conservatives. Liberals "trust" the government and would like to see it allocate more tangible services. Conservatives don't want to relinquish tax dollars or prerogatives to what they think of as an incompetent yet overly controlling nanny state.

Unity and modernity comprise the third group of properties. Unity, or shared history and culture in the past and shared purpose in the future, and modernity are the most recently conceived and most abstract of the nation-state properties; they are the *notional* properties of the nation-state. Sovereignty, boundedness and attribution are intertwined properties. Attribution and unity are also closely related. Law and order were conceived as relying on boundedness, and protection and provision are, in turn, dependent on law and order. Protection was the original reciprocal property of the nation-state and expanded to include provision for well-being.

The sixth and seventh properties are the most abstract and complex. I present the term "unity" in quotation marks throughout this book because examination of foundational texts supports this expected property, but also reveals that "unity" has multiple dimensions, which are contradictory as best and untenable at worst. These dimensions include a unity of history and culture for the people of a nation-state that extending into the past and unity of purpose and hopes that extends into the future.

## Sovereignty

The history of the nation-state can be said to be the history of the public, contractual, and functional definition of sovereignty. Though the nation-state was just emerging as a competitor to the empire when sovereignty began to be codified as a political idea, the notion of the sovereignty of comparatively small polities paved the way for the development of the nation-state. Each major language in which the concept of a nation-state has been discussed has a strong analogue for this word and concept: souveraineté, souveränität, soberanía. Romance, Germanic and even Slavic languages derive the word from the Latin *superanus*, meaning superior, chief, or principal. John Milton spelled the word "sovran," as though from the Italian "*sovrano*," a type of gold coin. However, both origins indicate high value or potency. In the version of the word with a "g," the first part of the word conveys superiority, and the second part, "reign," comes from the word root for rule or king: *Regnare* and *regnum*.

The idea of sovereign nation-states was put in writing with the Peace of Westphalia in 1648, which resolved a generation of sectarian strife between Protestants and Catholics. According to Anderson (1983/2006), the nation-state was subsequently conceived of as sovereign (during the rise of nation-states from the late 19th into the 20th century) because the right of the nation-states to escape external intrusion became necessary as empires fell apart. Additionally, the ideas of the Enlightenment were "destroying the legitimacy of the divinely ordained, hierarchical dynastic realm." (Anderson 1983/2006, 7)

The first practical application of the sovereignty established by the Peace of Westphalia was that the religion of the head of state determined the religion of the populace. However, this became a secondary meaning, and since the 17th century, scholars and politicians have understood sovereignty as the injunction against interference in a given nation-state's internal matters by political bodies originating from outside its boundaries.

It's not clear how this unwarranted expansion of the conception of sovereignty took place. Marxist theorists such as Eric Hobsbawm see the ascent of the nation-state (unchecked by other political institutions, such as a supranational alliance of nations, or the Catholic Church) as intertwined with capitalism. Habermas (2001) has explored how cultural identity contributed to the mythos and emotional urgency around self-determination and autonomy of the (German) nation-state. Anderson (1983/2006) has noted how emotionally compelling is the mythology of the nation-state state and this irrational appeal may have contributed to the momentum of any given Great Power (German, Great Britain, the Soviet Union, or the United States) running roughshod over the sovereignty of other nations while pursuing its own expansionist destiny.

The concept of sovereignty initiated with the Peace of Westphalia was not necessarily sovereignty for the "nation-state", per se. The word "state" appeared over 50 times in the treaty, meaning variously municipality, province, duchy, and kingdom. However, the word "nation" did not appear once in the document signed on October 24, 1648. Signatories represented a variety of polities, including the Holy Roman Empire, the Old Swiss Confederacy, Spain, France, Sweden, the city of Venice, what are now the German cities of Köln (or Cologne) and Freie Hansestadt Bremen (the Free Hanseatic City of Bremen), and the Republic of the Seven United Netherlands. Indeed, the very names of the various social structures—kingdoms, a republic, a confederacy, an empire and independent cities—demonstrate clearly that the nation-state was only beginning to emerge at that time. In signing the Peace of Westphalia, the entities agreed that they would commence noninterference with one another's civil matters and commerce, and that their own citizens would be granted (limited) religious freedom.[22]

The Peace of Westphalia appears to have introduced the idea of the polity as a legal person, with the prerogative not to be interfered with. This is something of a repetition of the monarchical legal principle that the King was the state. But the Westphalian vision was also consistent with assertion of rights of the individual *against* the state—the right not to be harmed or detained bodily.

This analogy of the polities to individuals can be seen in Section 118 of the treaty, in which states and other political entities, and individuals, whether religiously designated or not, are listed together—as legal equals to be treated in similar ways, i.e. to be given certain rights and protections, but also obligated to be obedient to the authorities:

> Finally, That all and every one either States, Commonaltys, or private Men, either Ecclesiastical or Secular, who by virtue of this Transaction and its general Articles, or by the express and special Disposition of any of them, are oblig'd to restore, transfer, give, do, or execute any thing, shall be bound forthwith after the Publication of the Emperor's Edicts, and after Notification given, to restore, transfer, give, do, or execute the same, without any Delay or Exception, or evading Clause either general or particular, contain'd in the precedent Amnesty, and without any Exception and Fraud as to what they are oblig'd unto. (Treaty of Westphalia).

Hobbes (1994/1668) famously asserted that the natural condition of human society and "the life of man [is] solitary, poor, nasty, brutish, and short." In order to attain protection he suggested that citizens should entirely subject themselves to the state, which will provide order and protection.

---

[22] The main concern at the time, however, seems to have been financial recompense for the damages of the prolonged armed conflict. This explains the length of the document, nearly 15,000 words.

In the *Two Treatises of Civil Government,* published after the Revolution of 1688 put William of Orange and Mary on the English throne, Locke (2008/1690) touted the right of citizens to rebel when they were mistreated. This laid the conceptual groundwork for the American Declaration of Independence's assertion that the populace may separate itself from its government given just causes.

The Scottish philosopher David Hume (2002/1741) wrote that people should revolt against only the most offensive abuses and favored tradition in setting social and legal rules. However, he also asserted that there is no natural right of governmental sovereignty that one polity can exercise over another; therefore, government should be based on a shared and consensual social contract. The next stage in the development of the theory of sovereignty was the formulation of the doctrine underlying the French Revolution.

Rousseau (1968, fp. 1762) advanced the concept of sovereignty by stating that it flowed from the plebiscite and their "natural rights"—claiming for the first time the citizens' role in granting authority to the government. Rousseau articulated this as the "general will," as distinguished from the will of the head of state. According to Rousseau, the general will, once established, is inviolable.

Kant suffered a special horror of the upheavals and losses of armed conflict. His work (1971/1784) shows an early articulation of ideas foundational to the League of Nations and United Nations. However, his ideas about a community of states grew out of his belief that the nation-state had absolute sovereignty over the individual. "The ruler in the State has against the subjects clear rights and no (enforceable or compulsory) duties."[23] (Cavallar, 1999) Even theories of the nation-

---

[23] Der Herrscher einer Staates hat gegen den Unterhanen lauter Rechte und keine Zwangs-Pflichten.

state that pre-date Weber are consistent with his definition that the government has monopolistic control of the initiation of force within a bounded territory. This derives from his 1918 lecture, *Politics as a Vocation.* (1948, 78). Weber asserts that "'sovereignty' is accepted as the essential attribute of the modern state, conceived as a 'unity,' while the acts of its organs are looked upon as instances of the exercise of public duties." (1948, 670)

Although there are numerous laws that pre-date the nation-state in allowing the individual to use force in self-defense, the state and specifically the nation-state is sovereign in that it currently holds a legitimated monopoly on right to *initiate* force within its boundaries. Being sovereign also dictates that other polities may not reach into the nation-state and dictate social or other practices—the issue over which the Thirty Years War was waged. It should not, or *should not without specific reasons,* (some of which are codified, some of which are tacitly understood, and some of which are flouted in international relations), interfere with other polities outside its boundaries. This simplistic idea of "what's outside is yours and what's inside is mine"[24] remained the dominant conception of sovereignty for three centuries.

Until the capacity for nuclear weapons, instantaneous communication, and transnational terrorism caused public intellectuals and scholars to note the degeneration of sovereignty, theoretical respect for this nation-state property was nearly absolute, though there are variations among early theorists of the state and variations among states because of their size, impoverishment, or domination by larger states. The point is not the practical infringements on nation-state sovereignty,

---

[24] "Mean" Joe Greene, an American football defensive tackle who played for the Pittsburgh Steelers in the National Football League (NFL), reportedly bit the finger of an opponent who grabbed his facemask (an illegal action under NFL rules). He later justified his action with this quotation.

but the statement of the expectation of sovereignty in legal documents and public discourse.

## Boundedness

Former Secretary of State George Shultz has said, "The revolution in global communications thus forces all nations to reconsider traditional ways of thinking about national sovereignty." The crisis may be in sovereignty and other expected nation-state properties, but it is the *loss of nation-state boundedness* that is creating the current monumental shift of political order that we now face.

Nation-state boundedness comes from the dual expectations that (1) a line can be drawn around a country, and (2) the government can control what happens inside that line. Historically, theorists and citizens expected boundaries to hold—for a nation's economy to be delimited by its boundaries, for walls or guard posts to stop threats at the border, and for a nation's culture to be defined within its borders. In the past generation, we have seen unstoppable flows (of money, ideas, drugs, weapons, workers) out of—and into—nearly every nation-state.

According to Anderson (1983/2006), boundedness is the most concrete property of sovereignty in practice. It refers to the outline of geospace and the expectation that the nation-state can keep resources inside or outside national borders. Weber similarly addressed boundedness as the territorial limitation of sovereignty: "a human community that (successfully) claims the monopoly of power of the legitimate use of physical force *within a given territory.*" (1948, 77-128)

Anderson cites as specific examples the emergence of Asian and other nations that "demarcat[ed] their exclusive sovereignty wedged[25]

---

[25] Anderson's elegant use of the verb "wedged" demonstrates an understanding that these nation-state properties are both a shared social fantasy and fraught with contra-

between other sovereignties." (1983/2006, 172). For example, he describes how new maps depicting Thailand directly and immediately affected Thai politics and political speech.

> [T]he new conception of spatial reality presented by these maps had an immediate impact on the vocabulary of Thai politics. Between 1900 and 1915, the traditional words *krung* and *muang* largely disappeared because they imagined dominion in terms of sacred capitals and discontinuous population centers. In their place came *prathet*, 'country,' which imagined it in the invisible terms of bounded territorial space. (Anderson, 1983/2006, 173)

Boundedness or designation of a geospatial area of control of the nation-state is deeply intertwined with sovereignty. From the 17th century through the end of the Cold War, the nation-state has been envisioned as having geographically contiguous territory within clear and impermeable boundaries. The right to noninterference within those boundaries is the defining Westphalian characteristic.

Writing at the end of the Cold War about the effect of the French and American Revolutions on the public conception of the nation-state, Hobsbawm (1990, 19) asserted that "The equation nation = state = people, and especially sovereign people, undoubtedly linked nation to territory, since structure and definition of nation-states so constituted, and this was indeed a necessary consequence of popular self-determination." Both in the Enlightenment era *about which* Hobsbawm wrote and in the early post-Cold War period *during which* he wrote, it was clear that the nation-state properties of sovereignty and boundedness were central to the conception of the nation-state.

Concurring with Anderson, Hobsbawm, as well as Sassen (1991), Albrow (1996), Gellner (1997), Nelson (1996) and Brenner (1999) cor-

---

dictions. The seven properties that I identify are simultaneously overlapping and in tension with one another.

roborate the *expectation* of this second characteristic of the nation-state—boundedness—while simultaneously noting its erosion. Gellner frames this erosion in terms of the boundedness of a nation's economy, stating:

> "The nation today is visibly in the process of losing an important part of its old functions, namely that of constituting a territorially bounded 'national economy' which formed a building block in the larger 'world economy,' at least in the developed regions of the globe. Since World War II, but especially in the 1960s, the role of 'national economies' has been undermined or even brought into question by the major transformations in the international division of labour, whose basic units are transnational or multinational enterprises." (1997, 181).

## Legitimacy, attribution at the nation-state level, and "recognition" of any given nation-state

The Weberian ideas of legitimacy, international lawfulness, recognition by other states, and a locus of responsibility comprise the third nation-state property. The history of the modern state can be read as the substitution of abstract rules for personal authority, culminating in Weber's concept of legality as legitimacy. The word root of legitimate is "law," but legitimacy is played out in international discourse through the word "recognize." Pakistan was the only country that officially *recognized* the Taliban when it entirely controlled Afghanistan. Only Russia recognized the independence of South Ossetia and Abkhazia in October 2008, while the world largely recognized East Timor in May 2002 and Kosovo in February 2008 at their moments of independence. The word used for the creation of these two new nations was "birth." Other linguistic metaphors of personhood abound.

To capture this idea of legitimacy and—more importantly—the role of the world political community in acknowledging the rightful government of a nation, I use the word "attribution." The opposite of legitimacy is delegitimation—or the loss of being viewed by the international community as lawful and justifiable in its actions. I do not believe that attribution is a nation-state property that needs to be reconceptualized. However, in my dissertation, I did find a widespread consensus among the writers that attribution at the nation-state level (rather than a non-state level) should be better fulfilled.

Attribution is pointing, publicly, to the source of the nation-state's responsibility and decision-making. (This responsibility and decision-making must have some potency. When such potency is lacking, as in Somalia, the entity may be referred to as a "failed state.") These qualities are grounded both in the construction of the state as a legal person—note the catalogue of political entities that were given status equal to legal persons under the Peace of Westphalia—and in concerns expressed by Hobbes (1994/1668), Locke ((2008/1690), Kant (Cavallar, 1999), and Weber (1948/1921) about the legitimacy of the state and the derivation of its right to power. Attribution of a state's authority is what Hobbes (1994/1668, 6) called the "Artificiall Man."

Contemporary statute positivism and normative theories both put forward the idea that eliminating ambiguity from laws would purge the state of arbitrariness. The bundle of ideas that I refer to for brevity's sake as "attribution" is perhaps the most invisible of the expected nation-state properties, but it is nonetheless crucial. Attribution began to be codified with the Peace of Westphalia. In the years preceding the legitimation of the nation-state, competing polities attempted to levy taxes and tithes and to enforce certain behaviors (such as religious practices), but could not be relied upon to provide unitary and unequivocal juridical decisions or military protection. From inside a nation-state, attribution is the "here" where the buck stops. In terms of the international state system, attribution is where President Merkin

Muffley's phone rings with bad news about a rogue plane loaded with nuclear arms.[26] The decision-maker's power on the other end of the line is far from unlimited but he or she is publicly known to have the authority to speak and act for the nation-state. This is a requirement that the nation-state system places on its member states, and the internal political arrangements of nation-states do usually satisfy this requirement. That there are exceptions, nation-states such as Somalia or even Pakistan that cannot speak or act for the unified whole only underlines that lack of attribution is a deviation from the expectation.

Attribution is particularly crucial for the nation-state. The political "body" is no longer embodied corporeally in a monarch, feudal lord, emperor, or pope, but rather is merely symbolized or represented through a head of state (but even in this turn of phrase, the synecdoche of a body part, the head is still used). Gone is the sense of divine privilege for the head of state that Louis XIV conveyed in *"L'état, c'est moi."* (I am the state). In its place is a set of rules to which a nation-state desiring to maintain its power must adhere. Nation-states are legitimate and accepted in a community of states because other states and their citizens say that they are. This is Weber's idea of legitimacy. Reason, and therefore a modernist conception of the nation-state, replaces what Weber calls charismatic authority.

Precisely because "the polity" cannot be seen or heard, it is necessary for a given nation-state to have a name, a single capital city, an executive, and an agreed-upon idea of the nation-state; it must have legitimacy or recognition that is not so gravely questioned that it cannot succeed. That Pakistan alone recognized the Taliban between the late 1980s and September 11, 2001 looms large in trying to make sense of the attacks on that date.

---

[26] As in the film *Dr. Strangelove* (1964).

The idea of attribution—of a single, agreed-upon point of authority for any given nation-state—is related to the concept of unity, the sixth of the nation-state properties that I address. However, attribution is the existence of a point of authority at the operational level, while "unity" or claims about unity pertain to the people, who supposedly share a 1) linguistic, cultural or historical heritage, 2) a political will in the present, or 3) a vision of good things that the future may hold.

## Protection and provision of social welfare to the citizenry

Writers with very different agendas (Nock, 1935; Spickard 1999) have differentiated between negative and positive action on the part of the state. The language can be counter-intuitive but Nock is saying that negative action by the state *stops* people from doing things (such as killing one another) while positive action allocates some good or services to people (Nock is opposed to this). Taking an entirely different tack, Spickard refers to first level, second level and subsequent levels of human rights. First tier rights correspond with negative action in Nock's parlance. People have a right not to be killed (and the government is supposed to enforce this right). Spickard asserts that people have subsequent tiers of human rights, such as housing, access to healthcare, etc.[27]

---

[27] In this formulation, the first tier of human rights starts with protection from bodily harm, as in early English Common Law. Later in history, but still at the first tier of rights are freedom of speech and freedom of worship. Freedom from want is a second tier human right in that it implies a covenant that the government will provide some physiological needs such as food, water, shelter, and clothing. Maslow, Nock, Spickard and other theorists from a variety of disciplines articulate this difference from the state's responsibility not to cause physical harm versus the state's responsibility (disputed by libertarians such as Nock) to support material and social well-being, i.e.

At the height of public agony over American military involvement in Vietnam, Richard Barnet wrote an editorial in the New York Times that underscores the normative expectation that the nation-state should protect and foster the well-being of its citizens—and that by expending resources in the armed conflict in Vietnam, it was failing to do so:

> The nation-state is obsolete. Because of radical changes in the world environment, the basic political unit around which international society has been organized for almost 400 years is no longer capable of meeting desperate human needs. The crisis is particularly acute for the large nations, which are increasingly unable to use their unparalleled accumulation of power to decrease the sum of human misery.
>
> The last three American presidents of the United States have candidly told the American people that the Government cannot defend them against a Soviet nuclear attack on the United States. It can only endanger them, making them hostages in power confrontations.... Barnet (1971, 27)

In my research, I found that—while writers increasingly perceive nation-states as failing to satisfy this vital function—they want the nation-state to meet this responsibility. Indeed, protection of and provision for the social welfare is arguably the most critical property to understanding 'the elephant as a whole.'

The notion of state protection of its citizenry through a mutually beneficial social contract can be seen in Hobbes (1994/1668), Rousseau (1968/1762), and Kant (Cavallar, 1999). While the duty of a state to provide material support—a "second generation" human right (Spickard (1999)—is *not* articulated in the American Constitution, both Bobbitt (2002) and Skocpol (1979) assert that the idea of a state's re-

---

food, shelter, clothing, education, sense of purpose, etc. (So-called third tier human rights include peace, economic development, and a clean environment.)

sponsibility to care for the plebiscite arose with the French Revolution. Skocpol (1979) examines how France, China, and the former Soviet Union were created in the crucible of internal collapses and external diplomatic crises. Protection of and provision for the citizens become additional and urgent raisons d'être of the nation-state, perhaps in part because they are the most visible and immediate functions of the nation-state.

Citizen protection is the obverse of sovereignty. Before the signing of the Magna Carta, the sovereign's authority was absolute. There was no discussion of King John's responsibility to provide justice or well-being. In fact, the sovereign's absolute power may well have conflicted with the protection of or provision for the nobles or commoners. Hobbes sought the abdication of public sovereignty precisely in order to gain protection from the state. John Locke in his *Second Treatise of Government* held that rationality leads people to enter social contracts for their mutual protection.

## Provision of laws, control and order within and between nation-states

In the writings I reviewed, the second most mentioned property of the nation-state (after attribution) was enforcing domestic and international adherence to laws. Writers' overall perceptions were that law and order, both inside nation-states and in the international community, declined during the period from 1946 to 2008. (Writers also conveyed a sense that metanational entities were increasingly violating stated precepts.) Like protection of and provision for citizens, the nation-state property of lawfulness does not need to be reconceptualized. It merely needs to be fulfilled.

Law, and who should create and enforce it, was a concern of countrymen Kant (Cavallar, 1999) and Weber (1948, 1968), with the former suggesting that only a community of states can enforce laws that also protect citizens, and the latter recommending a rational, procedural basis of law so that order and justice are not subject to the whims of the head of state. Hobbes suggests the citizen's subjugation to law as the vehicle by which to provide protection to the people of the society, mentioning God but not relying on the logic of the existence of God to afford sovereignty to the monarch.

Lawfulness—seen as the codification of social norms and expectations—is also a central concern of Weber's *Economy and Society*. Weber's goal is to demonstrate that the law is coming to be based in rationality, rather than a cult of personality, superstition, or dynastic privilege. Weber then explores the rationality and procedural specifics as a way to make the laws of the nation-state seem more just and less arbitrary.

Paul et al. (2003), Lentner (2004), and to some extent Hirst (2001) can be called "defenders of the nation-state," in part because they believe that the nation-state is the best social structure for law. It is the only macro social system with built-in mechanisms for representation, procedural justice, dissent, potential for reform, and external obedience to international conventions, they claim. In the view of the "defenders," citizens in a nation-state, and nation-states in an international system comprising checks and balances, are most likely to escape being crushed by social breakdown, mob rule, or totalitarianism.

Paul et al. (2003), Robb (2007), Soros (2000, 2002), Zakaria (2003) discuss the capacity of democratic societies to accommodate minorities, and the accompanying predilection in such free societies for minority groups to produce extremist or separatist movements, as well as the impulse both by and against minority groups toward "ethnic cleansing." There is a troubling contradiction here. Free society allows for the absolute antithesis of protection of minority rights and freedoms—

a political problem relevant to both the protection expected from the nation-state and the expected nation-state property of "unity."

## Unity

Nation-state "unity" has been conceptualized as designation of the state as a single legal person and unification of the consenting plebiscite into a single political entity. In this sense, it is related to the property of attribution and has roots in the Westphalian idea of polities as legal people. "Unity" also refers to the mythology of the unified ethnic, racial, and linguistic identity of the "nation," the ancestrally privileged citizens of the nation-state. In this sense, it appears in the King James Bible, not as a political unity but a people who share history, culture and destiny.

Weber's use of "unity" means decision-making power granted to the bureaucratic offices and executives that rule the nation-state. This is confusing because decision-making was quite deliberately split by the American Constitution and remains divided in modern constitutional system. The entire population does not, practically speaking, rule the entire nation-state. Nonetheless, political texts from the 18th century onward use the word "unity" and its cognates in other language to mean authority. This is, in part, why I place the word in quotation marks.

Weber principally explored "unity" in terms of a unitary point of law making and authority, although there is some (disparaging) mention of the purity of the "German spirit" (1968, 1405) as a unifying ethnic and linguistic identity. So, unity of decision-making is not practically the case, but there is an underlying meaning of the collective will of the people, or the prerogative of governmental and bureaucratic officials to act in the name of the will of the people.

Hobsbawm (1990, 18) corroborates the nation-state property of "unity" being central, particularly to the American and French conceptions of the nation-state, as expressed in the words "united," "union," "one," and "indivisible" in key documents. The American and French nation-states consciously characterize "unity" as consensus regarding the direction for the nation-state and voluntary participation of the citizens in this trajectory.

The emergence of the nation-state was painful for people in the Enlightenment era and this pain persisted through the convulsions of the Industrial Revolution and wars of the 20th century in large part because cultural norms and reference points were being discarded without being satisfactorily replaced. According to Anderson (1983/2006), the very newness of the nation-state as it facilitated the upheavals of capitalism and industrialism necessitated the creation of the mythology of an ancient, shared, unified history of any given cultural group as it coalesced into a nation-state. Anderson asserts that, during the age of nationalism, the nation-state was propagandized to be unified, precisely because it was not, and to have a long history, precisely because it did not. The exciting myth—the social construction—of unity helped persuade citizens to comply with the direction chosen by its leaders or government (even when, particularly when they were not in unity with such a direction).

Smith (1971/1983, 1996) is a theorist who has uncritically discussed the ethnic core of nation-states. He is sometimes referred to as an ethnosymbolist because of his attempt to synthesize modernist and primordialist approaches to the nation-state. As such, he wrestles with the conceptualization of nation-state "unity" in both the conscious and unconscious dimensions first identified by Kant (1971/1784). In response to a seminal essay by Renan (1994/1882) entitled, *"Qu'est-ce qu'une nation?"*[28] Smith and Hutchinson wrote:

> In a famous phrase, Ernest Renan declared a 'nation's existence' to be 'a daily plebiscite.' By his metaphor of a plebiscite, Renan was drawing attention to the psychological dimension of nationalism. Nations do not have an absolute existence, but without a 'clearly expressed desire to continue a common life the nation disappears into history.' The notion of a daily plebiscite suggests a psychology of the conscious will, rather as Benedict Anderson's later idea of an imagined community implies a psychology of imagination. In this respect, Renan's metaphor is somewhat misleading for literally, there is no conscious daily choice. The citizens of an established nation do not, day by day, consciously decide that their nation should continue. On the other hand, the reproduction of a nation does not occur magically. Banal practices, rather than conscious choice or collective acts of imagination are required. Just as language will die for want of regular users, so a nation must be put to daily use.
>
> The notion of a plebiscite also draws attention to the relations between nationalism and democracy. The nation, according to Renan, is chosen, rather than imposed: if the members of the nation reject the idea of nationhood, then the whole business of national community collapses. There is, therefore, an inherently popular, if not formally democratic aspect of nationalism. In democratic states, the national electorate has its chance every few years to express its collective choice in formal plebiscites. In between times, the sort of daily plebiscite that Renan had in mind solidifies into habitual routines. These routines include habits of discourse, enabling 'the people' to identify themselves, and thereby reproduce themselves, as 'the people'. As 'the people,' the electorates in liberal democracies at election times choose 'their' leaders and set the political course of 'their' national destiny. Smith and Hutchinson (1995, 1432-33)

Smith and Hutchinson's analysis conveys their idea of an unconscious, ancient cultural momentum of national unity that, though ever

---

[28] What is a Nation?

changing, nonetheless has a trajectory. Smith and Hutchinson assert that the nation-state (as a consensual if not completely unified social construction) is created through daily routines, including public discourse, elections, and decision points. The notion that public conversation 'creates' the nation-state supports the use of *perception* of nation-state properties to better understand its condition as a whole.

## Modernity

More recent political philosophy reflects the expectation of the nation-state as a product of modernity. This is most consistent with the school of political scientists of which Anderson (1983/2006) is a part. Anderson's thesis of the nation-state as an "imagined community" was central to my research (Redd, 2009a), as well as to my selection of the seven functions of the nation-state.[29]

Anderson explains how the nation-state came to be perceived as the organic and natural large-scale unit of society in the two and a half centuries following the treaties of Westphalia in 1648. Before the codification and imagining of the nation-state, the dominant macro social structures were religious and imperial dynasties, whose territories were noncontiguous and militarily controlled. Prerogative to rule over these religious and worldly empires was transferred ancestrally, often with a mythology of divine authority. In the 17th century, such empires became overextended, unwieldy, and fragmented.

––––––––––––

[29] The foundational political philosophers, Hobbes, Locke, Hume, and Rousseau use the word "modern," but not specifically as a property of the nation-state. The word is largely used consistently with its original entry into English from the Latin adverb "modus" meaning "recently." Each of the four philosophers addresses the newness of the social order, but not explicitly the nation-state as a *modern* institution, in the sense of its being intrinsically secular, rational and oriented toward commerce.

Anderson (1983/2006) posits that the nation-state is intrinsically modern, because it came to maturity in the Industrial Age and because of the values it has served—capitalism, maximization of profit, efficiency, mechanization, and rationalization.

Particularly with regard to theories articulated during the Cold War, thought on nationalism can be separated into three schools—primordialist, modernist, and postmodern (or postcolonial)—based on how the theory places the nation-state in social time. For example, Anderson (ibid.) sees the nation-state as having come into existence symbiotically with capitalism, making him a modernist. Pointing to millennia-old "nations" such as Egypt, primordialists see the nation as an institution that dates to antiquity and has inescapable racial and ethnic dimensions. Postmodernists (grouped here with postcolonialist theorists) question altogether the placement of the nation-state in time, attempting to sort through legacies of precolonial culture and colonial and imperial domination to come through to independence with a workable hybrid of history, identity, and functionality. The differences are most visible and will be noted most closely among the modernist theorists, principally Anderson, Hobsbawm, and Gellner.

The modernist approach is particularly evident among the works on nationalism written before the end of the Cold War.[30] Anderson (1983/2006), Gellner (1983), and Hobsbawm (1962) assert that the nation-state arose in conjunction with industrialism and modernity—

---

[30] Keeping in mind Geertz's point that political theorists necessarily reflect the concerns of their own time, communism and communitarianism were held out as viable alternatives to capitalism until the fall of the Soviet Union in 1991. For this reason, political scientists of the period wrote, in part, in opposition to capitalism. When one of the major embodiments of communism ceased to exist, however, globalization became a major focus of political theory, particular as the flow of investment, finished goods, raw materials, communication, and cultural artifacts across nation-state boundaries seemed to be eroding historical conceptions of nation-state properties.

emphasizing efficiency, rationality, technology, and capitalism. These three modernists are critical of the nation-state in this regard, asserting that the nation-state is not necessarily the best or most organic social structure.

The reason for this review of expectations about the expected properties of the nation-state is to attempt to respond to Bobbitt's assertion with which I start the chapter. What is the purpose of the nation-state? We can't argue with or update its purpose without laying out a clear statement of what it has been historically and how that has evolved.

Our ancestors (albeit unconsciously) imagined these properties. How useful do we think these properties are? What I call the "operational" properties of sovereignty, boundedness, and attribution? The most tangible (and later) protection-and-provision and law-and-order? And the abstract but compelling expectations of the "unity" and modernity of the nation-state? If the reader agrees that I have correctly enumerated these expected properties, how can we use these expectations, handed down to us, to shape a nation-state that is sustainable, useful and just?

In my examination of newspaper texts responding to crises and turning points of the nation-state, Modernity was the sole property that writers did not view as declining. That modernity remains a significant organizing property of a nation-state is best revealed in writers' responses to the September 11 attacks. When editorial writers found their voice after that Tuesday, they condemned the attacks as anti-rational and anti-secular—indeed, as anti-modern. However, in response to that event and others of the late 20th and early 21st century, they did not state that they saw the nation-state declining in modernity overall. I take up the modernity of the nation-state again in chapter ten.

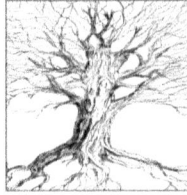

# CHAPTER FIVE. THE ENDURING NATION-STATE

Calling on the nation-state. Protection of dissent. International solutions. Insights via African independence processes.

\*

...[T]o re-invent states rather than to reject or circumvent them.

—Robyn Eckersley, *The Green State: Rethinking Democracy and Sovereignty* (2004, 3).

Hundreds of letters and editorials were written in response to some of the most momentous and alarming events transpiring between 1946 and 2008. These events included the founding of the U.N., NATO, E.U. and W.T.O. (these four being what I call metanational projects), collapses of nation-states (such as the Iranian revolution, the Bosnian Wars, and the implosion of the Soviet Union), attainment of independence by African, Asian, and Caribbean nations, and attacks by non-states against states, such as the events of September 11, 2001 and the war between Hezbollah and Israel during July 2006. By definition, these four kinds of events—projects superseding nation-states, regime changes, successful independence movements, and warfare waged by fractional political entities—are all *non-state* occurrences. Yet, the astonishing finding was that, during dire confusion and trouble, writers in the public sphere invoked the ideal of the *nation-state* as they tried to make sense of or offer advice about catastrophes and new actors on the world's political stage.

## Calling on the Nation-State

The predominant perception of the writers who wrote letters and editorials to three newspapers was that during political emergencies and transitions, in fact, *especially* during grave crises or major turning points, the nation-state was their point of reference for political procedure and efforts to pursue stability. Writers invoked the structures and conventions of the nation-state even while they communicated a diminishing belief that any given nation-state *was* satisfactorily meeting seven expected properties of nation-states that I outline in chapter four: Sovereignty, nation-state boundedness, legitimacy, etc.

The purpose of this chapter is to persuade the reader that the nation-state endures as the most promising political structure in the pursuit of inclusion, justice and stability. To a greater extent than any large social structure yet devised, the nation-state is capable both of inspiring enough cohesion for people to cooperate in pursuit of collective good, while providing mechanisms to protect people against too much governmental domination.

## Protection of Dissent

Habermas asserts, "[T]he idea that one part of a democratic society is capable of a reflexive intervention into society as a whole has, until now, been realized only in the context of nation-states." (2001, p. 60) By "reflexive intervention," Habermas means national course correction or social reform. In chapter four, I review classic scholarship on several central properties of the nation-state. Hume, Locke and other writers contemplating the purpose of government gave justifications for full revolt by the citizenry, in the face of abuse of their rights. However, these theorists about (pre-nation-state) government expected the options for citizens to be: 1) submit to domination, or 2) rebel and start over with a new state. They did not seek—because

81

there had been few examples of—ways for the people to peacefully influence the trajectory of a society as a whole (i.e., its population plus the government), the capacity for self-correction that Habermas touts.

The American, Canadian, Indian, South Korean and other Constitutions guarantee citizens' rights to criticize their government, to gather publicly, and otherwise work *within* the system for revisions of public policy.[31] Nation-states with provisions for free speech, assembly, and other forms of protest *are* able to (in theory) and do (in practice) accommodate dissent and social innovation with relatively little societal disruption. Neither empires, nor the corporations and other entities of the global economy, nor ideologically defined subnations currently provide such *codified* protections of disagreement and potential for changing existing power arrangements.[32]

Nor do these other social structures (empires, corporations, global financial institutions, etc.) have a program for sharing power among diverse groups and making decisions via representatively elected members of a congress or parliament. Protection of individuals and minority groups, whether ethnically defined or disadvantaged by virtue of material inequality, may be stated goals, but there is no *procedure* for democratically including their voices. Even the European Un-

---

[31] In fact, a great number of national constitutions, such as that of the People's Republic of China extend the promise of protecting free speech and the right to protest. This guarantee is not carried out in practice, as evidenced by the recent revelations of "black jails" to detain petitioners traveling to Beijing for redress of grievances.
[32] Though one can imagine such structures with highly elaborated protections—hybrids between macroregional or global structures and the protections of the (ideal) nation-state—the nation-state is the starting point for those hybrids. Several of the public intellectuals considered here, including Annan, Habermas, and Stiglitz contemplate such hybrids.

ion, as advanced a new political species as it may be, is only semi-democratic.[33]

Profound reminders of this point emerged in the texts responding cataclysms and transitions from 1946 to 2008. In the days following September 11, 2001, when Americans were still dumbstruck by the attacks on New York and Washington, DC, more than one unnamed contributor to the *Times of India* and the *Daily Gleaner* drew a connection between protest by Americans against their country's military involvement in Vietnam and the meaning of the September 11 attacks. Several made the point that citizens of the American nation-state had been *allowed* to disagree with their government's actions, that they had been formally protected by a document to which the government largely adhered. And this protection of dissent was an achievement to be honored. Except for the shooting of four students on May 4, 1970 at Kent State University, Americans had not been killed by their own government for voicing disagreement with its policies—as were Chinese students in Tiananmen Square in 1989 and Iranians protesting the results of the presidential election in 2009. One of the writers commenting on 9/11 from outside the U.S. exclaimed:

> If this was the America which went to war against Vietnam and unleashed the napalm bomb, this was also the country where thousands rose in protest against Washington's military atrocities. It was American civil society's conscience that stirred the world to follow its leadership in ending the Vietnam War. ("Paradox of America," 2001)

---

[33] The Treaty of Lisbon went into effect December 1, 2009 and states in Article 2: "The [European] Union is founded on the values of respect for human dignity, freedom, democracy, equality, the rule of law and respect for human rights, including the rights of persons belonging to minorities. These values are common to the Member States in a society in which pluralism, non-discrimination, tolerance, justice, solidarity and equality between women and men prevail".

For all the pain of American division over the U.S.'s involvement in a distant proxy war with the Soviet Union, the center held, and America was not wrenched apart. People were permitted to speak and to gather, and they were ultimately heard. This achievement of the American nation-state seemed worth remembering as the world contemplated the implied military and cultural reasons for the 9/11 attacks—American imperialism, bullying and decadence.

The connection that op-ed writers drew between the tragedy of 3,000 civilians killed by al Qaeda and the American nation-state's capacity to accommodate anger and protest was an intuitive one. "Why did this happen to America?" cried out the writer quoted above, citing other examples of civic and Republican spirit. Other speakers decried the way that al Qaeda expressed its rage, in bloodshed, when other modes were possible.

I have searched through the writings of sixteen public intellectuals, whose selection I enumerate and justify in chapter three. One of those, leader of the Liberal Party of the Canadian Parliament, Michael Ignatieff explored the equilibrium between security versus justification of emergency measures and limits set on government in *The Lesser Evil* (2004). The "lesser evil" is the manageable risk from asymmetrical attackers, while the greater evil is allowing security concerns to erode the nation-state's covenant of rational procedures and guaranteed protections for citizens. Significantly, Ignatieff's underlying assumption is that the principles of the nation-state are the most promising for holding the use of governmental force and intrusion in check while also guarding against threats.[34]

---

[34] This is also consistent with Darius Rejali's study of torture in its corrupting influence on the institutions of the torturing state.

As explained in chapter four, analysis of 555 opinion-editorial texts revealed that writers showed declining fulfillment of six of the seven nation-state properties (plus a nuanced perception of nation-state modernity). At the same time, qualitative assessment of the themes and metaphors used by the op-ed writers revealed a widespread belief in the unsurpassed potential of the nation-state to protect minorities and offer a program for sharing power.

## International Solutions

I looked for evidence of an emergent "postnational" world, but instead found that the world and its problems continue to be seen in terms of *national* problems with *international* solutions. By "international," I mean "among *nations*," rather than other entities. Writers talked about how diverse groups have thrashed out compromise within nations for eight generations, *and* how small and large, poor and rich, and democratic and undemocratic nations in a community of nations have tried and failed to resolve conflicts since the founding of the League of Nations and the U.N. The nation-state persisted as the model for international relations and for negotiating polyethnic and other conflicting demands.

Analysis showed that, while newspapers writers expressed a view that the seven nation-state properties were not being fulfilled, but they did not imagine or propose an alternative social structure that could do a better job than the nation-state. Instead, they called on the nation-state (both specifically and as an abstract institution) to fulfill those seven properties.

The indispensability of the nation-state's power-sharing process can be observed when diverse groups require a program attain consensus—even an uneasy consensus—in situations where the negotiators at the table simply can't get everything they want. For example, during the independence processes during the 1960s of the Democratic Republic of Congo (DRC), Kenya, and Somalia, there was a failure to reassure minorities and even substantive pluralities that they would be satisfactorily included in the government that emerged. The participants did not achieve enough of a coalition-building process, and, once the process became winner-take-all, the losers then worked for destabilization of the resultant government. A writer in *The Times of India* asserted that Congo's Patrice Lumumba and Joseph Kasavubu both vied to be the "big man," ("The Congo Mutiny," 1960), rather than considering what each might contribute to the process if he did not become the leader of the DRC. This is consistent with other systematic research (Roeder, 2007) showing that failure of new nation-state can be blamed on lack of inclusion in the overall consensus and stubborn factionalism during the independence process.

## African Independence Processes

Two points emerged from the newspapers' editorials and opinion pieces with regard to these African independence processes. The first was that the evolution toward African democracy was rushed in some cases, with inadequate provision for the inclusion of all competing factions. As Fareed Zakaria (2003) has written, majoritarian rule will run roughshod over disempowered segments of a society if they are not permitted to participate in power-sharing and protected by codified promises. The second point was that—where preparation for self-rule by majority was adequate—it was the nation-state's traditions and machinery of deliberation and negotiation among groups that incorporated disparate voices and distributed power.

Considering another African country, Sudan, An Na'im (and Deng) supported the use of nation-state procedures in their 2006 article, "Self Determination and Unity: The Case of Sudan." The authors asserted that national unity (by which they mean consensus) of competing ethnic groups in Sudan or other nations is possible when, but only when, all the groups can come together in a mutually respectful decision-making process. The authors examined the case of Eritrea and the breakup of Yugoslavia to determine principles by which power sharing and mutuality could have been more successful.

An Na'im and Deng argue that the deliberative processes of the nation-state will most successfully be coupled with the principles advanced by overarching metanational entities (particularly since Although nation-states have been the sources of all the principles subsequently advanced by metanational entities). They specifically cite guidelines for settling such disputes from the U.N., Organization of African Unity, and Cairo Summit of 1964.

It is fascinating to consider An Na'im and Deng's argument juxtaposed with Charles Taylor's *Multiculturalism* (1994). In a book-length essay, the Canadian philosopher Taylor pursues precisely the same conundrum of how to employ the particularity-blind capacity of the nation-state to treat competing parties equitably, while acknowledging ethnic or linguistic groups' desire for cultural self-determination. Rationality and procedures are touted as the way to resolve allocation and legal standards for competing cultural groups—but Taylor concludes that rationality and proceduralism are themselves culturally biased to favor the Western world, the colonizers, men, i.e. those who hold most of the political power.

## Nation-States and Metanations

If there is an emergent macro social structure to incorporate the nation-state, it will, by definition, consist of a set of stronger ties between the nation-state and metanational structures. Annan (2000/2004) asserts that the nation-state is a crucial champion and protector of its citizens as they are buffeted by global capitalism. Stiglitz makes a related point in *Making Globalization Work* (2006). He first describes the problem of globalization as the growth of an increasingly "informal" economy without formal rules to control it. "Formal" in this analysis means codified, based on a negotiated agreement such as a constitution. Stiglitz in both works (2003, 2006) says that globalization has great potential to enrich people and that he favors capitalism and competition in a free market. What he calls for is a "free" global economy in which wealthy countries are not protecting their own interests while forcing open the markets of poorer countries and in which there are not controls on short-term, profit-driven commercial activities that can ravage local commerce, agriculture, and ecosystems.

What is needed, Stiglitz says, is to attain a balance between market forces and governmental services, particularly economic ones, such as public pension programs, incentives for innovation and sustainable technologies, and protections for workers.

Stiglitz advances a number of concerns and recommendations. As he argued in *Globalization and its Discontents* (2003), the rules must be the same for advanced industrial countries so as not to further disadvantage people just entering the world economy. This is an argument for greater transparency on the part of metanational economic entities in their dealings with nation-states and was the point, if a single point can be drawn, of the W.T.O. protests in Seattle in December 1999.

Stiglitz asserts that there is a need for better measurement of values that are currently not monetized very well, such as social cohesion, traditional cultural patterns, and long-term prosperity. The analogy to ecosystems in nature is an apt one. If unfair competition drives traditional economic activities into extinction, entire communities can be destabilized, as we have already seen where cash crops set up by outsiders have driven out established crops and trades, and then family and unrest have followed. Similarly, Zygmunt Bauman has raised the concern that, as economic globalization increases, community, meaning, and human connections become road kill in the quest for a better bottom line (2004).

Finally, though Anderson (1983/2006) explains how the Euro-Western model of the nation-state was transplanted to Asia, Africa, and South America, Stiglitz and Zakaria (2008) both caution that globalization must not automatically be Americanization. Forcing Western, specifically American, values of individualism, efficiency, workaholism, etc., on developing countries can be damaging, perhaps irreparably so. In Stiglitz's view, the problem is that *economic* globalization has outpaced *political* globalization (and comfortably-paced cultural adaptation to either). To Stiglitz, the solution is a political one: representation, equity, and power sharing must be reallocated to developing countries now trying to participate in the global economy. Developing countries may not be strong enough to force this change, Stiglitz notes, suggesting the value of metanational organizations that can advocate on their behalf.

## Postnational Prognostications

In chapter two, I offered a survey of prognostications for a postnational world. As money, goods, information, and people began to pour across national boundaries during the 1980s, scholars and other public intellectuals began to predict the decline of sovereignty, boundedness, attribution, protection, provision of well-being, lawfulness, unity, and modernity. Rosecrance was one of the first to predict the emergence of what he called the "virtual state."

Significantly, even as writers predicted the weakening—and even demise—of the nation-state, they continued to describe it in terms of the seven properties I have identified.[35]

## State-Centered Scholarship

State-centered literature includes classic theory on "nationalism"[36] written before the end of the Cold War; this was followed by a loosely associated school of thought called postcolonialism (which has some overlap with globalization theory). It was penned by professors of the humanities and other thinkers who were contemplating how former colonies should conceive their versions of the nation-state.[37] These theorists included Arjun Appadurai, one of the 16 public intellectuals I chose for this project. These writers are deeply exploratory and literary

---

[35] Considering whether there are other operational, reciprocal, or notional properties of the nation-state affords a test of the completeness of the list of nation-state properties. One such property is democracy or representation of the plebiscite in the governing process; however, this possibility can be refuted in part by noting that, of 192 member nation-states in the U.N., fewer than a quarter can be considered free and democratic (Fassihian, Darnlamian, Patel, and Piccone, 2007). Taking this into account, "nation-state" would either have to be defined differently than the way it is outlined by the U.N. or democracy must be omitted from the list of nation-state properties.

The leanness of the list is open to debate. There is a large overlap between sovereignty and boundedness, but they are not identical. Anderson (1983/2006) emphasized the *limitedness* of the modern nation-state in contrast to its political predecessor, the empire, which had a distinct center and blurry outlines. There also is substantive overlap between the meanings of attribution and "unity" because attribution means point of responsibility and authority. However, the word "attribution" captures the Weberian idea of legitimacy in a way that "unity" does not. Law-and-order and protection of and provision for citizen likewise overlap in meaning, but law and order conveys international adherence to law whereas protection and provision are services provided to the citizenry.

[36] Please see the discussion of "nationalism" in the Glossary.

[37] Important writers in postcolonial theory include Albert Memmi (1965), Gayatri Chakravorty Spivak (1988, 1998, 1999, 2004), and Edward Said (1979).

in their approaches. However, they continue to talk about the nation-state, because they grew up in nation-states with lasting influences from the colonizers. Memmi wrote not only about the psychological cost to members of a colonized or formerly colonized country who come to believe that their own culture is inferior to Western culture, but about the rotting effect on the colonizer, as well (an assertion supported by Darius Rejali's (2007) work on the corrupting effects of torture on the institutions of the torturing state). Appadurai (1996a, 1996b) considered how globalized media replicate memes—some of which are poisonous to traditional identities and patterns—while Spivak explored how minorities and suppressed groups can make themselves heard in the political arena.

Sovereignty, nation-state boundedness, unity, and modernity—four fundamental properties of the nation-state—need to be reconceived. The machinery of the nation-state remains capable of taking into account dissenting voices and resolving conflicts, in a way that no other institution yet can. This is not to say that non-profit organizations, universities and scholarly association, transparently and ethically functioning corporations, and religious alliances do not *also* have a role in easing people into a more just and inclusive manifestation of globalization. They do. It's simply that the dimensions of the constitutional republic provide a covenanting and a way to integrate disparate voices and needs more explicitly than any of these other institutions. The balance of this chapter explores the view that the nation-state is indispensable, as gleaned from the letters and editorials I examined in the dissertation research, as well as the works of the supplemental group of 16 living public intellectuals.

It not only matters that the public intellectuals I have chosen use the nation-state as their point of reference, but it also matters how they categorize the nation-states in the international community. George Shultz and Zbigniew Brzezinski alternately categorize the world into allies and threats, the U.S. and everybody else, or the West and everybody else.

In broad strokes, Abdullahi Ahmed An-Na'im (2008) can be said to categorize nation-states into "modern" and theocratic. Building on a careful consideration of both secular and religious law, he concludes that the former is indispensable to protecting religious practice. From the standpoint of his own personal faith, An-Na'im argues for abandoning the very idea of a theocratic Islamic state. He asserts that such states have undermined religious choice and sincere religious practice in trying to enforce Shari'a, the Islamic law governing every aspect of how people should conduct their lives. He cites Koranic verse to support his arguments that (1) there can be no compulsion in religion, and (2) Shari'a should be thought of not as an explicit code, but as a process of legal reasoning, a point also made by Kofi Annan (1999b).

In a state-centered analysis that nonetheless emphasizes *evolution* of the nation-state, Robert Cooper (2003c) categorizes international community as pre-modern (unstable or dysfunctional states like Somalia or Afghanistan), modern (narrowly self-interested but stable and powerful states like the U.S. or China), and postmodern (cooperative states with transparent operations and some sacrifice of sovereignty to metanational organizations, like Japan and the E.U. members). It may well be that Japan's and the E.U.'s interconnected evolved because they were merely taking advantage of the U.S. security presence after WWII. Nonetheless, Cooper says that what they became is a useful model for how the nation-state can effectively cope with globalization.

Thomas P.M. Barnett divides the world into the "functioning core" (subdivided into the "old core" and the "new core") and the "non-functioning gap." The "old core" category includes the U.S., U.K., E.U. members, Japan, and other developed nations. The "new core" consists of countries with formidable economies that are nonetheless not wealthy and not necessarily democratic, but are engaged with and desire to be more engaged in the global economy; countries in this category include India, Russia, Brazil, Argentina, Chile, Mexico, China, and South Korea. Finally, the "non-functioning gap" includes largely equatorial countries that have suffered the ravages of colonization, are torn between (often religiously expressed) tradition and modernity, and are generally poor and unstable. Between the "core" and the "gap" are "seam states" that must contend with largely Islamist terrorism and other destabilizing factors. "Seam states" include Mexico, Morocco, Algeria, Greece, Turkey, Pakistan, Thailand, the Philippines, and Indonesia, among others. (2005, 212-213).

## A Renewed Nation-State

I began this chapter by sharing my astonished encouragement that hundreds of writers had pointed to the nation-state as the best scheme in town—or at least the source of the "least worst" future—for self-regulation, inclusion, negotiation among competing or clashing international factions and interests. But how can the ideal of the nation-state as an operating system for sharing of power and protecting of subgroups be put into action?

If I am correct, the nation-state, though revamped, will endure, and people will continue to call it the "nation-state." After all, what I am calling the expected nation-state properties became more brittle and absolute over the first three hundred years of the life of the institution. I am suggesting that the nation-state be completely transformed, only that its components become more pliable and useful to the trends at hand.

The Westphalian nation-state with its conceptions of absolute sovereignty, impermeable boundaries, racial purity, and the unsustainable modernity of national-industrialism *is* defunct. However, these

93

four properties of the nation-state can and should be rethought and reformulated so that globalization—with all of its associated opportunities and peril—can be accommodated under the aegis of the nation-state.

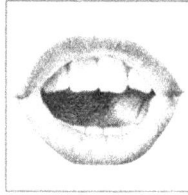

# CHAPTER SIX. IN THE WORDS OF

The research question. How four families of predictions about world order corresponded to opinion-editorial texts. Turning points for the nation-state. Critical discourse analysis.

*

[L]anguage...is not merely a reflection or expression of social processes and practices, it is *part* of those processes and practices. For example, disputes about the meaning of political expressions are a constant and familiar aspect of politics. People sometimes explicitly argue about the meanings of words like *democracy, nationalization, imperialism, socialism, liberation or terrorism*.

—Norman Fairclough in *Language and Power* (2001, 19).

Jürgen Habermas arrived in Manhattan in early October 2001, three weeks after the twin towers had been reduced to a smoking hole. He said later in an extended interview (2003, 26), "[T]here [was] a widespread awareness of living at a turning point in history."

Every one of us lives through shocks, losses, ceremonies, validations, and epiphanies that are remembered afterwards as momentous—a fulcrums for making meaning so that life is retroactively divided into before and after that event (e.g., "after my father died," "before I met my husband," and "after I gave birth to my daughter"). Some are private signposts for an individual, a family, or a community; others are broadly felt and deeply shared. Like Habermas, I also experienced a shift in the months and years after September 11, 2001, as did many of us.

Did the use of four planes as missiles signify a rough beast slouching toward Bethlehem? Or was it merely the most pyrotechnic sign of seething anger of which the public had previously been only dimly aware? What would happen next, as vague advisories and ambiguous alerts—blue, yellow, orange—were issued?

This chapter explains the methods employed to try to find some answers to these questions and the larger, overarching uncertainty: what transition, if any, is underway in social organization on a grand scale?

## The Research Question

The following were the research questions: How can a fundamental shift in public perception of social structure (if there is one) be discerned? What is the nature of the shift? Is the nation-state giving way to something else? The answers to these questions continue to resonate, and are the underpinnings of this book. My research included reading approximately 60 books and articles (mostly written from the early 1990s through the end of the 20th century) to find out and categorize what "postnational" meant to popular writers and scholars. In chapter two, I presented a summary of these writers' predictions about the trajectory of world order. This is also presented as a chart of the objects of analysis of the research in this chapter.

The "non-state" predictions of world order included a resurgence of tribal, religious, and ethnic separatism and violence, a return to something like imperial control, social structure motivated by a desire to participate in the global economy, and ranging views about how globalization will affect people's lives—from increased local poverty to unprecedented macroregional cooperation.

## Objects of Analysis

Table 1 (below) shows how I coded the data consisting of the newspaper texts. The letters and editorials interpreted for my doctoral research mapped to state-centered *and* non-state predictions in the following way: Ethnocultural identity corresponded to texts commenting on the actions of politically relevant non-state actors, predominantly motivated by threats to their cultural identity (in many cases because of upheavals of globalization). The phrase "politically relevant non-state actors" also corresponds to my discarded hypothesis about "virtual nation."

The objects of analysis in the scholarly and popular treatises starting in the early 1990s were the four families of predictions: 1) ethnicity, 2) return to empire or some other form of control, 3) upheavals of globalization, or 4) the global economy. The objects of analysis in the newspapers were the events themselves that loosely fell under these four headings. To select the newspaper texts, I first selected 19 "event clusters" that organized the events to which writers responded. I discuss this further below under the heading, Turning Points for the Nation-State (see Table 1 below).

Generated out of concern for control and order at a higher level than the nation-state, predictions about empire and emergent changes in global order connected loosely with writing about metanations (such as the U.N., NATO, E.U. and W.T.O.), as well as with concerns about "globality" and planetary sustainability. There was very little discussion of metanational organizations in the first set of data. The articles and books had titles that emphasized panic in response to the Bosnian Wars as well as other indicators that the center (the nation-state) would not hold: *Pandaemonium: Ethnicity in International Politics* (Moynihan 1993), *The Coming Anarchy* (Kaplan 1994), *Nations without States: Political Communities in a Global Age* (Guibernau 1999), and

"The world in pieces: Culture and politics at the end of the century" (Geertz 2000).

Though some writers advocated something like a new empire to control the frequently mentioned "chaos" and "breaking nations" few of these works emphasized *other* metanational structures (such as the U.N., etc. mentioned above). One of the few that did came later. Brzezinski (2009) argued on behalf of strengthening NATO in Afghanistan and called for deeper commitment beyond Europe on the part of its members. However, this (prescriptive not predictive) article was not included in my original set of data.

Some could argue that there is a gap between the discussions of empire-like control in books written after the end of the Cold War and discussion of metanational projects in the 62 years of newspaper texts. This could be seen as a kind of failure of imagination of writers during the 1990s. Brzezinski's (2009) article is one of the few that bridges this gap. Clearly, international order supported by NATO is not the same as the replacement of indigenous governance by empires maintaining colonies, but there are some similarities in that standing armies would be a crucial part of control originating above the nation-state level.

The data set of newspaper texts begins with the founding of the United Nations (January 10, 1946), which brought with it nearly ecstatic hopes for its power to bring peace, even world governance. One reason that metanations did not figure more prominently throughout 62 years of newspaper texts is that the major metanational project after WWII—the U.N.—was invalidated—within months into 1946 by the deadlock over the Soviet Union's postbellum occupation of Azerbaijan. There continued to be loss of confidence conveyed in the letters and editorials because of the U.N.'s vacillation in compelling bellicose members of the international community to respond to the complaints of other nation-states. Editorials in all three of the news-papers conveyed acrid disappointment ("Monstrous failure," 1948, "Eritrean knot," 1950, "Solution for Eritrea," 1950, "Challenge to the U.N.," 1955, "Sad end," 1974). The hope intermittently arose that the U.N., as a metanation, *could* rise to the task of being the next domi-nant social structure, but was frequently dashed. By the late 1940s and into the 1950s and beyond, writers alternated between an accusatory tone and pleading for the U.N. to decisively address world controver-sies. The point here is that the U.N. did not end up being the metana-tional successor to the Westphalian nation-state that some might have hoped, at least as reflected in letters and editorials in the three news-papers that I reviewed over 62 years.

Comments on both the potential benefits and destabilizing effects of the global economy occurred throughout the editorial writing. Ap-peals to the nation-state to do its job and assertions that it is the most promising authority for keeping order (even during the Bosnia Wars, and other waves of independence, secession and collapse) also threads through hundreds of the texts.

## Turning Points for the Nation-State

The newspapers I selected for my dissertation research were the *New York Times, Times of India* and *Daily Gleaner* (of Jamaica). I dis-cuss later in this chapter why I chose these three.

Full text search was not available in the newspapers from India and Jamaica and was available to only a limited extent in older archives of the American paper. Therefore, to select the texts, I chose a set of events—like the fall of the Berlin Wall, the collapse of the Soviet Un-ion, and the attacks of September 11—that were shots across the bow of the nation-state.

To these, I added events relevant to metanational-global social organization, e.g., the founding of the U.N., the founding and milestone actions of NATO, the founding of the E.U. (and other stepping-stones of its predecessor organizations), and the founding and milestones of the W.T.O.

I also added event clusters—those that British sociologist Martin Albrow (1996) would call concerns of "globality." These included: (1) the Universal Declaration of Human Rights, shepherded by Eleanor Roosevelt in 1948, and selected subsequent human rights-related events, such as the revelation that the U.S. had conducted waterboarding on at least three al Qaeda suspects; (2) revelations of nuclear capabilities and attempts at nonproliferation and disarmament; and concerning (3) global warming and climate change. These event clusters about human rights and planetary survival were not intended as an exhaustive list, but rather as highly visible accords or crises to which op-ed contributors responded (and in doing so, revealed their assumptions about which macro social structures to rely on).

The third set of event clusters included regime changes (such as the Iranian Revolution in 1979, the dissolution of the former U.S.S.R. into 15 republics, and the dissolution and reconfiguration of former Yugoslavia), and the independence of several selected nations (including the secession of Eritrea from Ethiopia, and the independence and partitioning of India, Pakistan, Bangladesh, the DRC, Somalia, Kenya, and Jamaica).

In this third set, I also included texts responding to the final years of American military involvement in Vietnam, the Soviet occupation of Afghanistan, and the U.S. invasions of Afghanistan and Iraq.

**Table 1. Concepts Found In Popular and Scholarly Treatises After the Cold WarIn 555 Texts in Three Newspapers 1946-2008**

| | |
|---|---|
| Ethnocultural Identity | (How to Control) Politically Relevant Non-state Actors through cultural understanding |
| | Empire and Imperialism |
| Empire | Metanational Projects |
| | (How to Control) Politically Relevant Non-state Actors through military control |
| | Empire and Imperialism |
| Upheavals of Globalization | Concerns about Planetary Sustainability and "Globality" |
| | Upheavals of Globalization |
| | (How to Control) Politically Relevant Non-state Actors |
| Global Economy | Global Economy |
| | Concerns about Planetary Sustainability and "Globality" |
| | (How to Control) Politically Relevant Non-state Actors by understanding how they are affected by the global economy |
| State–centered predictions | Nation-State Transitions |

Finally, I chose a set of watershed events concerning the actions of non-states, such as the Palestine Liberation Organization (PLO), its successor Fatah, Hamas, Kurdish independence factions, Hezbollah, Tamil separatists, and al Qaeda.

In sum, I chose a range of what might be called "turning points" for the nation-state as an idea and an institution, and I used these turning points to select the "data" in the three newspapers.

In reviewing the relevant literature, I identified seven properties of the nation-state. (As I explained in chapter four, the properties of sovereignty, boundedness, attribution, protection of and provision for the citizenry, provision of law and order, unity, and modernity have been consistently expected of the nation-state.)

The method I used for the dissertation is called critical discourse analysis; I actually counted words referring to the seven nation-state properties and determined whether, in that specific mention in a letter or editorial, the writer thought that a property (e.g., sovereignty, protection of and provision for citizens) of a given nation-state or nation-states in general was being satisfied.

## Critical Discourse Analysis and the 16 Public Intellectuals

To conduct the doctoral research, I counted words (and main concepts to which words pointed). In the subsequent research involving the 16 public intellectuals I traced etymologies and looked for references to evolving nation-state properties. I do continue to rely on the premises of critical discourse analysis that 1) a given writer may not be fully conscious of the metaphors and assumptions in his or her thinking, but that 2) these are nevertheless reflected in the language choice and analogies used. Furthermore, language does not only reflect arrangements of power: it helps create them.

The recent research turns on the following four properties of nation-states: sovereignty, boundedness, unity and modernity (and their adjectival forms). As I discuss in chapters seven and ten, "sovereignty" and "modernity" are highly recognizable nouns, with clear etymologies and few synonyms that carry as much weight. All four of the words come originally from Latin roots, but "boundedness" (or "boundary") from Old French *bodne, bodina, butina* for boundary marker, possibly influenced by *bonnarium* for piece of land and "unity" have many, many synonyms in common English usage. This chapter is intended to make my counting and interpretation of all four concepts more transparent to the reader.

Metaphor and analogy are central to this book, which is why I start each chapter with an image. As we learned in junior high English class, a metaphor is a comparison (without use of the words "like" or "as") between two things that are intrinsically *unalike* in most respects, but share a few important underlying properties. The literary device of metaphor  allows us to consider the deeper and nonobvious natures of things.

Analogies, meanwhile, are comparisons of pairs of things that are intrinsically similar: A is to B as C is to D. The device of analogy lets us use language to discern the nature of things by conceptually placing them beside other things which may share several characteristics or contexts.

However, when hidden analogies are embedded in our language, we need to be careful. Use of analogies can have unintended consequences. One example is the analogy of communities to living bodies. I.e., a brain is to a body as the president is to the nation-state. The person considered as a part (a cell or an organ) of a political *body* (or ecosystem) is a pervasive and problematic motif in political discourse. Bodies as a whole *do* function as totalities. However, as such, living bodies are fundamentally *totalitarian*. Neither eye cells nor colon cells get to choose their jobs, and both can—without moral compunction—be wholly sacrificed to the greater health of the body.

An analogous sacrifice of the individual by the body politic is, however, not justifiable. Each human being (or cell, in the analogy) has a value that must be respected, even when the "cell" is sickly, deviant, or incapable of the same level of productivity.

In order to keep the brain and heart warm, our warm-blooded bodies cut off circulation to extremities if we are suffering from hypothermia. However, applying an analogous remedy to the body politic in times of economic or other national hardship is clearly abominable. The healthy body succeeds by sloughing off cells that are no longer useful. But whether a "healthy" (note the hidden analogy) community is in fact a "success" should be judged in part by how well it treats the sick, useless, and troublesome members of its body politic. [38]

Because the specific terms "boundedness" and "unity" were seldom used in the texts of the 16 public intellectuals, I found it necessary to look for a nebula of ideas surrounding the underlying concepts. For example, the word "unity" does not appear at all in Appadurai's *Fear of Small Numbers* (2006), and "unified" appears just once (and refers not to unity of a nation-state, but to the unity of Hindus against other factions in India). Thus, I came up with other words that suggest and relate to the concepts of nation-state boundedness and "unity." These words are listed in chapters eight (boundedness) and nine (unity).

The point is that language—choices of words, shades of meanings of words, combinations of words, and the pictures painted by words— actually affect how we understand the phenomena to which those words point, and affect how those phenomena or policies become social reality for all of us.

---

[38] See Rawls, John. *A Theory of Justice.* Cambridge, MA: The Belknap Press of Harvard University Press, 1971.

In the chapters that follow, I advance my own recommendations for reconceptualizing the nation-state—specifically its properties of sovereignty, boundedness, unity, and modernity—drawing on the work of the 16 public intellectuals.

# CHAPTER SEVEN. WHAT NOW FOR SOVEREIGNTY?

A solution to a problem. Many meanings since Chaucer. Sovereignty as non-intervention. Absolute sovereignty. Postwar perceptions of diminishing sovereignty. Exceptions to sovereignty—preemption of danger and humanitarian intervention. Special cases of sovereignty. The future of sovereignty.

\*

[N]ations dream of being free.... The gauge and emblem of this freedom is the sovereign state.

—Benedict Anderson, *Imagined Communities: Reflections on the Origin and Spread of Nationalism* (1983/2006, 7).

Why in mid-June of 2009 did Russian President Dmitri Medvedev serenely host Iranian President Mahmoud Ahmadinejad at a regional economic summit while hundreds of thousands of Iranians were protesting the outcome of an Iranian presidential election that may have been stolen from reformer Mir-Hossein Mousavi?

And what motivated Venezuelan president Hugo Chávez to voice support for the Iranian incumbent (Ahmadinejad)—even as violence against bystanders in the streets of Tehran seemed to be going terribly wrong?

One could argue that the answer is lack of respect for human rights, or the common desire to oppose the United States, or the common interest of oil producers. Yet, the ideal of sovereignty also plays a role in the unfolding of these events.

Sovereignty is an emotionally charged word. Sovereignty is the nexus of mediation between the power of one entity and the self-determination of another. Understanding sovereignty, what it has been and what it may become, is at the very heart of this treatise.

Sovereignty was—and continues to be—precious to Iranians, Russians, and Venezuelans, as well as to other statesmen and citizens—public and private. In June 2009, the world watched the unrest in post-election Iran. And Iranians knew that the world was watching: the hand-lettered signs held aloft by supporters both of President Ahmadinejad and of his challenger appeared in English, French, and Spanish as frequently as they did in Farsi. The Iranian protesters knew that the informational boundaries separating Iran and Anglophones, Francophones, and Latinos were permeable at best. They had written their placards for the eyes of the free.

For their part, having witnessed regime-change in neighboring Iraq, the rulers of Iran feared that governments of the West might intercede once state-sanctioned violence against their own enraged citizens had begun.

President Obama interpreted the actions and words of Presidents Medvedev, Chávez, and other heads of state as the Iranian electoral crisis unfolded. Responding to the events after the presidential election, he invoked the "S" word, saying, "The United States respects the sovereignty of the Islamic Republic of Iran and is not interfering with Iran's affairs." ("President Obama's Press Briefing," June 23, 2009).

Sovereignty is the foremost property that people, professors, and politicians expect from the nation-state. This is because sovereignty was the first way in which dominant institutions (the feudal estate, principality, kingdom, empire, etc.) ceded power to the nation-state.

Benedict Anderson (1983/2006, 7) wrote about how people and leaders *re-conceptualized* dominant political institutions in the 17th through 20th centuries to serve changing needs, saying, "[The nation-state] is imagined as *sovereign* because the concept was born in an age in which Enlightenment and Revolution were destroying the legitimacy of the divinely-ordained, hierarchical dynastic realm."

In this chapter, I explore the many meanings that "sovereignty" has had. This etymological re-cap will form the basis for suggesting that re-thinking the meaning of "sovereignty" might further international stability.

## A Solution to a Problem

In the 17th century, the empire—whether Mongolian, Holy Roman, or Persian—no longer commanded public confidence. It had become overextended, unwieldy, and fragmented. From nobles to merchants to peasants, inhabitants of overlapping political entities struggled with contradictory demands and redundant taxation by their burgs, duchies, kingdoms, or religious institutions. Sometimes laws conflicted, or there was no decisive arbiter for settlement of grievances. The paradigm of empire, with its permeable, poorly defined boundaries and contradictory authorities, was breaking down at many levels.

The 16th century was a time of devastating ideological, political, technological, and social upheaval in central Europe. In 1517, Martin Luther posted his 95 theses of criticism of the Catholic Church on the door of the castle church in Wittenberg, Germany. At the same time, another Protestant group, the Anabaptists, were in an uproar in lower Germany and the Netherlands. Outside Germany, the Holy Roman Empire tightened its grip around dissenting Protestants. There were breakdowns of clear order and authority in central Europe and beyond.

After thirty years of sectarian strife over religious practice and control, the Peace of Westphalia resolved a generation of war.

The text of the two treaties referred to together as the Peace of Westphalia (2008) uses the word "sovereign" or "sovereignty" nine times. One reference is to the "Prince and Sovereign Count of Neuschaftel," but the other eight references guarantee that polities may control defined territories. Furthermore, the accord places *very* diverse political entities on equal footing with one another. Political scientists and historians say the treaties codified the phenomenon of sovereignty, a concept that had begun to play a role in the late Medieval morass of feudal estates, duchies, city-states, principalities, and empires competing for the rights to exact taxes and control territory.

Sovereignty was a solution to the problem of empire because it furthered what was already emerging—a community of distinct, self-directing, mutually recognized, territorially-contained polities.

The words "sovereignty" and "sovereign" are highly recognizable words, translating as cognates in many Indo-European languages, Russian included. However, the word "sovereignty" has changed dramatically in meaning over the past eight centuries. Its use in Middle English, Early French, and Medieval Latin meant *personal* power or social standing. The word was used during the emergence of the nation-state to refer to political *non-interference*, which even then was relational, not absolute.

## Many Meanings Since Chaucer

Because of the range of meanings of "sovereignty," it is useful to survey what it has meant in different eras. This lays a foundation to consider how writers may be reconceptualizing nation-state sovereignty today.

From Medieval Latin texts and from the word's usage with its Early French/Middle English spelling of *sovereynete* (illuminating its word root *super* meaning "above"), we know that the common usage of sovereignty was *not* associated with public authority before the 12th century (Kreijen 2004, 27). Furthermore, the Latin *superanus* is inherently relational, referring to one entity being higher with respect to another.

The three greatest writers in the English language afford us a snapshot of "sovereignty" in its pre-Westphalian connotations. When Chaucer's "Wife of Bath" uses the word in the Prologue to her tale (written in the 14th century), it is with the meaning of *personal* self-determination. The Wife tells the other Canterbury pilgrims that she knows from experience what women—wives—most want from life: they want "sovereignty"—a degree of control over their husbands and over their own lives.

Chaucer's colorful widow means this on an individual level. She is not referring to the self-determination of a social or political body. Further, both her first person use of the word, and that of her characters', reveal that she means this control on the part of the wife in her story *in relation to* her husband and to social norms (the honor of the husband).

Two and a half centuries after Chaucer wrote *The Canterbury Tales*, Shakespeare used the word "sovereign" in *King Lear*, spelling it with the "g" of Modern English. The word conveyed the title character's (waning) *personal* self-command or competence (1882, 82).

Fifty years after Shakespeare, John Milton spelled the word "Sovran" in *Paradise Lost*, using it in reference to the power of God *in relation to* the mutinous angel, Satan. Milton's spelling of the word may have been influenced by the Italian coin, *sovrano* or *sovranno*, conveying potency and value.

This etymological sketch reinforces my point that the properties of the state can be hidden metaphors for the faculties of human beings; this is further borne out by my linguistic analysis of the text of the Peace of Westphalia in chapter four, showing that the document laid the groundwork for a social construction of the state as a fictitious person, what Hobbes called an "Artificiall Man." (1994/1668, 6) My point here is that the substantive evolution of the word "sovereignty" should influence how we view its future trajectory.

Today the personal connotation of "sovereignty" has been subsumed by an almost exclusively political meaning of the word. Furthermore, it has come to mean *control* of the interests of a nation-state (rather than not being controlled by outside forces). This expectation of control is not absolute, but does extend beyond national boundaries. Objections to codified international cooperation from the North American Free Trade Agreement (NAFTA) to adherence to emissions standards, from fishing limits to nuclear arms reduction, are frequently framed in terms of loss of American "sovereignty." Strictly speaking, none of these agreements, which are by definition entered into voluntarily, entail international interference in American political self-direction, but they may require curbs on U.S. "interests." The word "interests" has come to have great weight in the interpretation of the actions of powerful nation-states, and defense of such interests is sometimes asserted in terms of threats to sovereignty. This asymmetry must be corrected for the international system to function.

## Sovereignty as Non-Intervention

In the modern age of nation-states in an international state system, sovereignty has variously meant non-intervention, freedom *to* intervene (interestingly, the opposite of the first item on the list), control, and the singular sovereignty of the American nation-state. Exceptions raised to the principle of sovereignty have included preemption of risk, humanitarian intervention, and emergent ideas such as shared sovereignty. As people, things, abstractions, and threats traverse nation-state boundaries with increasing volume at greater velocity, mutually conveyed[39] sovereignty, sovereignty-with-responsibility, or integrative sovereignty may become fruitful reconceptions of the concept first committed to writing in the Treaties of Westphalia in 1648.

Today, we seldom talk about an individual being "sovereign." The most prevalent connotation of "sovereignty" in today's parlance is political, and it usually refers to Westphalian non-intervention, not the absolute interpretation of sovereignty that sabotaged the League of Nations. It is also in this sense of non-interference with any given nation that the word "sovereignty" has been employed in subsequent U.N. resolutions.

A vestige of the personal metaphor persists, however, because it is part of public discourse to refer to the "will of the people" or even the "will" of a nation, illuminating the persistent mythology that a collective or polity can have a unified intent. I discuss this further in chapter nine.

During the 20th century, the connotation of "sovereignty" was expanded to convey a nearly absolute national right of self-direction and imperialism on the part of Great Powers—including the contradictory prerogative to *violate* the sovereignty of other nations. The League of Nations allowed its members to retain the ability to unilaterally declare war (seen as a prerogative of sovereignty). The League's inability

---

[39] Mutually conveyed sovereignty becomes an increasingly important idea in the public discourse—particularly near the end of the Cold War. It means (with the nation-state personified), "I recognize you and your authority, and you recognize me, but we have agreed on where my power starts, and yours stops, or where we overlap." I believe this is an important part of re-defining sovereignty in the age of international interdependence and globalization.

to supersede this "sovereignty" of member nations—including those that withdrew from League membership in the 1920s through the early '30s—led to its decay and eventual official disbandment in 1946.[40] Only one year later, in 1947, President Truman's "doctrine" began with his decision to intervene in the Greek Civil War. This proxy conflict with the Soviet Union was followed by proxy conflicts in the Korean and Vietnamese civil wars, with the rationale that these Asian nation-states should not be allowed to succumb to Communist rule. In all three cases, the argument was that the Communists had violated the sovereignty of the proxy nation where the conflict was being played out. *Preemption* of the perceived threat of the Soviet Union was part of the reason for American intervention.

## Absolute Sovereignty

In the years that followed WWII, the word "sovereignty" was appropriated to meant the unfettered exercise of will on the part of powerful countries. This may have been driven by rising fear of nuclear exchange between the two superpowers.

This was true not only of the U.S. and Soviet Union, but other colonial powers as well. In an unsigned editorial in *The Times of India* ("A Challenge to the U.N.," 1955), the unidentified writer asserted that France was touting her "sovereignty" to rebuff pressures to cede to the independence of Tunisia and Morocco.

---

[40] H.A.L. Fisher, a British Cabinet minister who became an Oxford professor wrote *A History of Europe* (1938), "If the nations want peace, the League gives them the way by which peace can be kept. League or no League, a country, which is determined to have a war, can always have it." The League was weak with no membership of the United States and betrayal by Italy and Japan, complicated procedural rules, all within a requirement that its decisions had to be unanimous.

Political philosopher Bertrand de Jouvenel decried the absolutism connoted by "sovereignty" during the 20th century. He criticized the way in which Great Powers placed themselves above internationally agreed-upon rules and claimed legitimacy based only in force. To Jouvenel, this was an extension of the conceptualization of sovereignty first articulated by Hobbes, in whose "horrific conception everything comes back to means of constraint, which enable the sovereign to issue rights and dictate laws in any way he pleases. But these means of constraint are themselves but a fraction of the social forces concentrated in the hand of the sovereign" (1957, 197).

The absolute sovereignty that so repelled Jouvenel parallels the often arbitrary "might makes right" credo that has been used to guard American interests. Johnson (2000, 2004, 2006), Sullivan (2004), and Harvey (2003) criticize this misappropriation of the concept of sovereignty in American foreign policy. Their assertions include the warning that the American Republic is degenerating into an empire—cruel, unprincipled, and morally and financially untenable.

One branch of meaning of sovereignty is what has become the intermittent perspective of some American presidents that combines absolutism regarding American sovereignty—reflected in, for example, an unwillingness to sign treaties banning land mines or reducing greenhouse emissions—with a universalism about moral standards that it uses to justify meddling in the affairs of other nations.

First defending and later criticizing America's "imperialist isolationism," Brzezinski (2005a) has noted the singular sovereignty of the U.S., stating that it is different from the sovereignty of any other polity on planet Earth. He writes:

> America's military action against Iraq and its less dramatic but also largely solitary stance on the International Criminal Court and the Kyoto Treaty were striking assertions of the unique status of the United States as the last truly sovereign state.... [T]he undeniable re-

ality of America as the sovereign power of last resort still begs the question: Sovereignty for what? Doubtless many would answer: for the sake of America's national security. But that reply begs a deeper question: Might not efforts to perpetuate America's unique status as an unconstrained sovereign eventually come to threaten America's national security, and its civil liberty as well?

Writers such as Ignatieff (2005a, 2005c) and Zakaria (2008) have also raised the issue of American exceptionalism and hypocrisy excused as "sovereignty." And their assertions dovetail with Ignatieff's (2004a) assertion that excessive force cloaked by concerns for national security and "sovereignty" can actually damage security.

American bullying framed as sovereignty takes the form of lack of regard for the sovereignty of *other* nations. Pepe Escobar (2006, 2009) interprets the presidencies of Hamid Karzai in Afghanistan and of Benazir Bhutto's widower Asif Ali Zardari in Pakistan as evidence that those two countries are not sovereign, but rather are under the control of the U.S. His broader concerns about the sovereignty of smaller and less powerful nation-states are articulated as concerns about the intense pressures of global capitalism.

## Post-War Perceptions of Diminishing Sovereignty

This survey of the use of the term "sovereignty" over the past several decades is meant only to underscore that "sovereignty" remains a verbal landmine—even among liberal scholars who may not have been big admirers of the nation-state in the first place. Beginning in the late 1980s, writers noticed something happening to the nation-state. Walls—both political and technological—were tumbling in the last quarter of the 20th century, and many things were crossing borders they could not cross before. I discuss these things—people and other living things, resources, commodities, money, and ideas—in chapter eight.

When the field of "globalization theory" emerged, scholars posited that, in its era of preeminence, the nation-state had enjoyed a confluence of government and society, but a "delinkage" between the two was now underway. Albrow (1996: 113, 158, 199, 241).

Essentially, the problem was too much freedom. Whereas people were once limited to jobs and other economic activities to which they could travel, now they could trade with anyone they could reach by telephone or Internet. Businesses could seek comparatively cheaper labor, raw materials, and phases of product assembly and storage on any continent. Intangible products like music, movies, pornography, subversive or controlled ideas, and other information could cross nation-state boundaries along with the other streams of electrons, and there wasn't much any nation-state—now matter how rich, populous, or powerful—could do about it.

This ungluing was happening between people and traditional institutions such as nation-states, but also between people and neighborhoods, communities, and sources of employment. Appadurai (1996, 27, 46, 189, 199) pointed to "disjuncture" among peoples' views of reality, their sources of identity, and the locales of their residence, their livelihood and the authorities that controlled them. Giddens (1990: 14, 21, 24, 29, 37, 64, 113, 120) went so far as to assert that there was a "distanciation" between *space and time*. He postulated that new technologies and the mobility of people eliminated traditional spatial and temporal constraints and enabled changes in social bonding, political loyalties, work, planning, and recreation.

A perception of the possibilities and new social patterns of globalization resulted in alarm bells—particularly from academics but also in public discourse. Some of these alarms were sounded in terms of perceived loss of nation-state sovereignty (Redd 2009a: 97-98, 114-115): that is, the loss of nation-state *control* over flows of people and goods, stimulated by the global economy. At the same time, concern was expressed in the public sphere over loss of protection (from the nation-state) over potential threats originating outside national borders. From 1946 on through the Soviet Union's first nuclear weapons tests in 1949 and for the remaining duration of the Cold War, much of the popular discourse on loss of sovereignty in the *New York Times, Times of India*, and *Daily Gleaner* turned on the capability of Intercontinental Ballistic Missiles (ICBMs) to cross nation-state boundaries.

Transnational commerce also increased during this period; in the editorial texts, this development was generally remarked upon as a variation on the evolving "unboundedness" of the world in the 1970s, and was labeled "globalization" beginning in the 1980s. These two phenomena (expected nation-state boundedness versus unboundedness or globalization) were expressed using the list of words for limits historically imposed by the nation-state that I list at the beginning of chapter eight.

Zygmunt Bauman gave an analysis of nation-state sovereignty in an interview (Bielefeld, 1993) that is still searingly accurate. He said:

> Contemporary neoliberalism is in part the product of the fact that the holy trinity of the traditional nation-state, economy, political and cultural sovereignty, is dissolving. Economic sovereignty is dissolving upwards into the European institutions, into multinational companies, etc. Indeed the state has only a limited economic sovereignty. At the same time it is losing its cultural sovereignty as it is no longer very interested in cultural homogeneity, in assimilation, in unifying. This is dissolving downwards into the market, into the groups, the ethnic minorities. What is left is pure political sovereignty without economic or cultural support. And this is what makes today's nation-state so weak. There is probably no power which could organize an industrial action like the Holocaust. On the other hand there is plenty of space for 'tribal' violence.

Writing about transnational commerce in *Losing Control? Sovereignty in an Age of Globalization* (1996a) and *Territory, Authority, Rights* (2006), Sassen (1996a, 1998, 2006) identified what she calls "global cities," in which service workers' transnational ties began to be stronger than their allegiance to the host nation. Her list of global cities includes New York, London, Tokyo, Buenos Aires, Bangkok, and Mexico City. In these metropolises, high-level knowledge workers conduct business with colleagues in distant continents, while low-level workers (often also transnational) serve high-level workers' needs—such as cooking their food, driving cabs, baby-sitting their children, etc.

The most cogent explanation of the injustices that have ensued as global commerce has outpaced political processes comes from Joseph Stiglitz (2006, 8). He cites a statement by the World Commission on the Social Dimensions of Globalization, which the International Labour Organization established in 2001. The Commission found that people becoming poorer because of globalization are caught in "[an] informal economy without formal rights." This is, in my view, the greatest failing of the nation-state to date, and the area most in need of rethinking. I frame this later in terms of the nation-states needing to follow their own rules.

A third realm of transnational activities was the social freedoms and capabilities that steadily expanded during the 1970s, 1980s, and beyond. Appadurai explored this expansion of the imagination and identity in *Modernity at Large* (1996a). These expanded possibilities include lawful and productive social, creative, and cultural activities (such as easier and broader access to media products), but they also empower unlawful and deleterious activities.

As I discuss in chapter eight, Appadurai's more recent book, *Fear of Small Numbers* uses a vertebrate-cellular analogy to explore the concept of "sovereignty." He contrasts established political structures in the globalized world ("vertebrate" social structures) with small and unregulated "cells" of terrorists, black marketers, and others who dodge the strictures and formal structures of the once-mighty nation-state. In this analogy, Appadurai interprets "sovereignty" as control of the body politic and its functions—control that is eroded with regard to activities of globalized non-state actors.

## Exceptions to Sovereignty—Preemption of Danger

Even before the Soviet Union tested a nuclear weapon on the steppes of Kazakhstan (an imperially held territory) in August of 1949, public discourse revealed ruptures in the formerly tough shell of the nation-state. Four years earlier, President Truman had approved the mission to drop atomic bombs on civilian populations. This degree of force implemented against one nation seems to have had an effect on the expansion of the conception of "sovereignty" over the decades that followed.

Since the first detonations of nuclear bombs, additional dangers have crossed nation-state boundaries—gases generated in one place that distort weather systems in other places, planes used as missiles on September 11, 2001, and horrors spilling across boundaries from Rwanda, Bosnia and Herzegovina, Somalia, and Afghanistan. A number of statesmen and public intellectuals, including Shultz (1985, 2006, 2007b) and Brzezinski (2007a) argued in favor of preventing danger to the U.S. by preemptively intervening at the perceived source of the threat.

Dangers that can cross nation-state boundaries have two dimensions of relevance to the meaning of sovereignty. The first is the loss of the nation-state's ability to control—that is, to shield its own plebiscite from—clear and present threats. The second is the preemption of future dangers. Both are used to justify expansion of Westphalian expectations of non-intervention.

Barnett (2004, 2005), Robb (2007), and Aslan (2008) have all discussed the end of the era of head-to-head war between sovereign states struggling to hold a piece of territory. Instead, they theorize, war will become "asymmetrical" as non-states strive to destabilize, delegitimize, and disrupt the infrastructure of nation-states. This is relevant to preemption because non-state actors still need to operate from some piece of geospace; this reality explains the U.S.'s entry into Afghanistan in an attempt to get at al Qaeda. (President Bush also justified the invasion of Iraq—at least in part—by insinuating that Saddam Hussein *might* have been harboring al Qaeda.)

## Sovereignty as Separation

The 20th century and the first decade of the 21st have seen an astonishing wave of newly independent nation-states. By one measure 86 new nation-states came into existence between 1941 and 1990.[41] In this period of decolonization, "sovereignty" meant "independence" or pulling away from the "mother" nation-state, so to speak. The vast majority of new nations created or transformed in that half-century declared independence from imperial dominators. Most also used ancient ethnic identity, at least partially, as a mobilizing impetus to become independent.

For example, political separation was the goal of the Liberation Tigers of Tamil Eelam (LTTE, also commonly known as the Tamil

---

[41] The exact number depends upon how one counts countries with populations below 250,000 and how one interprets the aftermaths of military coups d'état and changes of country names. Roeder (2007) draws on Gleditsch and Ward (1990) to count new and transformed nation-states in various waves since 1815 and discusses criteria for what counts as a nation-state.

Tigers). The Tamils are a linguistic and ethnic minority of Sri Lanka and the Indian state Tamil Nadu. (Malaysia, Singapore, and Canada also have significant Tamil populations). The reasons given for wanting to politically separate from India and Sri Lanka include lack of sufficient political representation in larger countries and a history of perceived oppression on ethnic grounds.

Tamil separatists are the infamous innovators of some of the first suicide bombings in history—in July 1987, in response to the Indo-Sri Lankan Accord. (Tamils were excluded from the negotiation of this Accord.) Tamil Eelam was the name they gave to the sovereign state they hoped to create on the northeast coast of India's southern neighbor, Sri Lanka.[42]

There is a disturbing confluence between popular understanding of sovereignty—particularly in this meaning I have been discussing—and separatism. And separatism, in turn, is related to the atavistic desire for ethnic unity or purity, which I discuss in chapter nine. The desire for ethnic groups—whether Francophones in Canada or Sikhs in India[43]—to have "sovereignty" within the larger, multicultural nation-state suggests perhaps that the majority has failed to provide sufficiently for minority resource allocation and self-governance, but also insufficient acknowledgement of or cultural respect for the subgroup. This lack decrease the ability of the minority to participate in decision-making alongside those culturally (dominant) and different from themselves.

---

[42] Their leader Velupillai Prabhakaran, was killed in May 2009, and Sri Lanka has declared victory in the military struggle to compel the Tamil separatists to remain part of the island nation. Tamil Eelam has ceased to be geospatial likelihood, though nation-state aspirations continue to be shared through www.eelamweb.com.

[43] For thoughtful discussions of how these two cultural groups have interacted with their respective nation-states, see Taylor (1994: 52-56) and Appadurai (2006, 46).

In March of 2008, South Ossetia (a region at the top center of Georgia) and Abkhazia (also in Georgia, but farther east and north)—both on the Russian border—called for "sovereignty." For a few tense days in August 2008, the idea of sovereignty as separation played out in a war between Russia and Georgia. In an attempt to weaken their influence, Josef Stalin[44] had intentionally split Ossetians between the then-Soviet provinces of Russia and Georgia. Dividing ethnic groups was good for the whole—the "unity" of the Soviet Union—albeit distressing—and tragic—to the ethnic groups themselves. Along with 13 other former republics of the U.S.S.R., Russia and Georgia became nation-states between 1991 and 1993. What had been sketchy, not-terribly-clearly enforced provincial lines became international boundaries. When the Russian-speaking, Eastern Orthodox, culturally more-Russian-than-Georgian Ossetians of South Ossetia wanted to separate from Georgia, President Medvedev was quick to recognize their "sovereignty," while Georgia was unwilling to lose a piece of its territory and population (even if South Ossetia had been awarded to Georgia relatively recently under a terrible dictator).

After crushing the Georgian army, Russia "recognized" the separatist regions of South Ossetia and Abkhazia as independent, a position deplored by nation-states including France, Germany, and—interestingly—Kosovo, itself only recently "recognized" as independent, the youngest nation-state to emerge from the dissolution of Yugoslavia. In April 2009, Russia signed a border deal with Abkhazia and South Ossetia, validating their prerogative to police their own boundaries, but leaving the matter in dispute with Georgia.

Arjun Appurdai (2006) finds this intersection of the concept of the nation-state and ethnic purity—played out in northern Sri Lanka and

---

[44] Né Iosif Dzhugashvili, from Georgia.

the Georgia-Russia conflict of 2008—very disturbing. Specifically considering the relationship of the "sovereignty" of minorities (such as Sikhs) in relation to the overall state, he argues that the expectation of nation-state "unity" is the root of violence against ethnic minorities. I discuss the entangled meanings of nation-state unity further in chapter nine; my point here is to note that the urge of subgroups to pull away from a majoritarian population is one of the important connotations of "sovereignty."

## Humanitarian Intervention—an Exception to Sovereignty

Political separatism, which almost always has racist or ethnicist origins, can lead to ethnicized violence. Systematic racially-, religiously-, or ethnically-motivated killing seems particularly repugnant, and raises the question of if and when outsiders should intervene to stop mass killings occurring *inside* the boundaries of another nation-state. Michael Ignatieff has special insight into this dimension of sovereignty and the exceptions to sovereignty raised by powerful nation-states such as the U.S. and U.K. He served on the International Commission on Intervention and State Sovereignty (ICISS), which released its *Responsibility to Protect* report in 2001. Ignatieff's essay, "Human Rights, Power and the State" (2006), explores the arguments for intervening in cases of human rights abuses or genocide. Ignatieff acknowledges the *realpolitik* behind "intervention" (specifically, the decision to remove Saddam Hussein's regime), and he asserts that Great Powers may make the argument that human rights are being violated by a tyrant, but they only intervene when it serves their larger purposes. Other human rights violations may go unchecked.

In a change of stance from his earlier works (1993, 2003) supporting interventions such as the American-led intervention in Iraq, Ignatieff

(2006) defends the lack of perfect consistency in intervening in humanitarian crises, because intervention is not always possible or successful, but not being able to always do so should not stop mediators from *ever* doing so. Ignatieff acknowledges that it may be difficult to determine from the outside what constitutes systematic human rights abuses that call for overruling the government of the nation in which they are taking place.

While Cohen (2008a) has called for a broader policy of intervention during humanitarian crises, Ignatieff is exquisitely cautious in this most recent statement. He does not assert that *all* abuses justify violation of the sovereignty of *all* nation-states. Ignatieff is aware that to intervene opens a Pandora's box of questions, such as how to offer a stable replacement to a despotic government.

Mahmood Mamdani shares Ignatieff's caution in the case of justifying intervention. Mamdani is the author of *Saviors and Survivors: Darfur, Politics, and the War on Terror* (2009). Just as "sovereignty" is a hot button, Mamdani says that framing the murders in southwestern Sudan in terms of a *moral* atrocity, without recounting the history of climate change and colonialism there, simply polarizes the situation without offering a solution. Mamdani cautions that labeling the killings "human rights" violations demands intervention. However, he says, outside intervention will only position perpetrators as dishonored criminals and survivors as punishing victors, engendering more slaughter in the future.

Mamdani's point about not describing killings in absolute moral terms (but rather in historical, political and sociological terms) could form the basis of a more humane and informed policy in cases of internal group–on–group or government–on–group persecution. Until 1995, conflicts in the Balkans were "ended" by outsiders with no true resolution and a cycle of violence that seemed unending. To put it another

way, labeling an act "genocide" eradicates the possibility of a negotiated political solution, for who can negotiate compromise with *any*
degree of "genocide"? Weighing the discourse by Cohen, Ignatieff,
Mamdani, and others on the use of "human rights violations" to justify
interference with nation-state sovereignty, I have come to the conclusion that the term "human rights" can be too polarizing. As columnist
John Leo (1993) has said, use of the word "rights" stops the conversation: once one party asserts that "rights" have been violated, the other
party is viewed as being completely in the wrong.[45] As soon as one
group asserts victimhood or higher moral ground there is no room for
negotiation and compromise. After all, how can one compromise the
fulfillment of "rights," which—by their political and linguistic history—come from beyond this earthly plane?

I am not diminishing the gravity of abuses against Bosnian Muslims, Albanians, Rwandans, the Sudanese, or others. I only suggest
that there may be other ways to *talk about*—and therefore resolve—
killings inside nation-state boundaries. What if, as Habermas has suggested in a number of works (Habermas, 1990; Passerin d'Entrèves,
1996; Habermas, 1998), social protections and prerogatives were conferred by citizens upon one another and codified in constitutional provisions?[46] If this were the case, then crimes could be evaluated in the

---

[45] The conservative reply is that dialogue about "rights" must always also include dialogue about "responsibilities." Notably, President Clinton produced some notable
successes in creating workable compromises around entitlements versus accountabili-
ty.

[46] Given that the constitutions of some nation-states already define rights and particularity-blind protections, the project is then to understand how this "Western" and
universalist covenant can lead to a more global covenant. This is precisely the work
that An-Na'im (2002, 2008), Habermas (1969/1971, 1981/1984, 1985/1987, 1987, 1996,
1992, 1998a, 1998b and 2001), Ignatieff (2006) and Taylor (1989, 1991, 1994, 2004 have
tried to do—explore a way in which equal status can be maintained while contending
with cultural differences of subgroups.

context of what happened and what rules it violated, with compensation and punishment meted out accordingly. Granted, there are nation-states with constitutions quite different from those of the U.S., India, France, or Canada—or no constitutions at all. Nonetheless, taking a step backward—literally and figuratively—from internal nation-state matters might make responses to abuse less heated and might also allow polities to own their own crises. Even in the case of total social breakdown, dispensing with "rights talk" might still serve justice better, as outsiders would embark on mediation and partnerships with other nation-states as equals, rather than intervene in a way that treats them as children unable to run their own affairs.

## Special Cases of Sovereignty—Shared Sovereignty

Absolute stances and absolute definitions—of rights, sovereignty, and control of territory—need to be re-thought.

I have nonetheless found some intimations in public discourse of *shared* (or what has also been called "pooled") sovereignty. And there are some actual political examples, as well. "Shared," "pooled," "transparent," "conditional," or "negotiated" sovereignty may be the next stage for sovereignty, solving some of the problems of absolute or Boolean sovereignty.[47]

---

[47] "Suzerainty" is one term for this gray area. It was a medieval power arrangement that allowed feudal holdings to be internally self-directing while surrendering fealty to a dominant polity. Several colonies of the Ottoman Empire, including a region of Southern Romania called Wallachia, the principalities of Moldova and Serbia, and Lebanon had suzerainty. By many definitions, the Native American territories of the U.S. and Canada are suzerain—they rule themselves, but are ultimately subject to a higher government. The suggestion of "suzerainty" in the case of shared control of territory might meet with fervent objections, however, demonstrating just how emotionally charged "sovereignty" continues to be.

This evolution of sovereignty has precedents in the negotiation of peace in Northern Ireland. The six counties of the Irish province of Ulster remained part of the nation-state known as the United Kingdom of Great Britain. At the same time, Northern Ireland retained a great deal of self-determination. Under the Belfast Agreement of 1998, citizens of Northern Ireland may hold Irish or British passports or both, as they choose. Refinement of Northern Ireland's self-determination has also entailed "devolved" national administrations for Northern Ireland (as well as for Scotland and Wales). Another example of implementation of shared sovereignty is in the Brčko district of Bosnia and Herzegovina.

Nor should we forget that the U.S. itself provides a fine example of relational sovereignty, though its political arrangements between the federal and state governments are never referred to as "devolved," nor is state (as in the State of California) "sovereignty" much mentioned (with the exception of the occasional civil war over "states' rights"). Legislation and taxation vary enormously among the 50 states, and there is an ultimate arbiter in the Supreme Court to draw and re-draw the line between federal and state authority.

Folklore and the Hebrew bible relate the story of wise King Solomon, who knew—in the dispute over a baby—that the mother who loved the child would never allow him to be divided into two pieces. The maturation of the conceptualization of sovereignty may prove indispensable in affording solutions in the case of territories so ancient and precious to cultural groups that they cannot be cleanly partitioned. The idea of sharing Jerusalem as the geospace for two capitals, with Jewish neighborhoods falling under Israeli sovereignty and Arab neighborhoods under Palestinian control has been offered as "shared sovereignty." The first appearance of this idea is credited to George Shultz (Lukács (1992), Quandt (2005: 271), and Shultz (1993, 454-7)), with subsequent advancement of the idea by Zbigniew Brzezinski

(2007). George Mitchell, who played a role in mediating the Peace of Northern Ireland, may advance this concept of shared sovereignty in the Middle East in his new role as U.S. special envoy there.

## Reconceptualization of "Sovereignty"

In the public sphere, and in most of the work by the 16 public intellectuals that I studied, sovereignty is discussed as national control or the right of non-interference. It is articulated either in terms of leaders asserting their sovereignty, or urging other nation-states not to interfere, or expressing fears of impaired sovereignty. They express these sentiments either because of the actions of other nation-states or—as is happening more and more frequently—because of uncontrolled activities that fly below the radar of nation-states. These uncontrolled activities, carried out by what Appadurai calls "cellular social structures", include asymmetrical political violence, unsanctioned flows of workers and monies, and "gray" or "black" markets.

The best hopes for reconceptualizing sovereignty into something more workable in a globalized world have come from Robert Cooper, Michael Ignatieff, and Javier Solana. Jürgen Habermas has also explored the evolution of nation-state sovereignty.

## The Future of Sovereignty

The problem with freedom is that everyone else has it too. In an unbounded world, the "sovereignty" of nation-states and the technologically enabled capabilities of non-state players on the world stage make it necessary to reconsider nation-state sovereignty.

The German philosopher Immanuel Kant worried about the popular conception of absolute sovereignty more than three centuries ago. In his essay, "Idea for a Universal History from a Cosmopolitan Perspective," (1874) Kant asserted that relations *among* nation-states need to be resolved in order for internal state justice to work:

> The problem of establishing a perfect civil constitution is dependent upon the problem of a law-governed external relation between states and cannot be solved without having first solved the latter. What good does it do to work on establishing a law-governed civil constitution among individuals, that is to organize a commonwealth? The same unsociability that had compelled human beings to pursue this commonwealth also is the reason that every commonwealth, in its external relations, that is as a state among states, exists in unrestricted freedom and consequently that states must expect the same ills from other states that threatened individuals and compelled them to enter into a law-governed civil condition. Nature has thus again used the quarrelsomeness of humankind, even that of the large societies and political bodies of this species, in order to invent, through their inevitable antagonism, a state of peace and security.

In the excerpt above, Kant is saying that "unrestricted freedom" or absolute sovereignty of states is dangerous because if individual nation-state are truly sovereign in this extreme way, then there is *nothing* to bring them under control when either their internal or external actions are brutal and unjust.

At a conference on the lingering relevance of the Peace of Westphalia, Javier Solana, then Secretary-General of NATO, said "humanity and democracy [were] two principles essentially irrelevant to the original Westphalian order," and asserted, "the Westphalian system has its limits. One of these is that the principle of sovereignty that it relied on produced a basis for rivalry, not community of states; exclusion, not integration." (1998, 1)

"Community" and "integration" are the two most important words in Solana's statement, and they are emphases of another important thinker who has helped to reconceptualize sovereignty. Robert Cooper (2003, 27-37) expanded upon Solana's insight, exploring how the international norm of *balance-of-power* transformed into *cooperation*. Before a paradigm of cooperation and transparency was developed, the only way to control a great power gone awry was for other countries to team up against it and balance its power with their own. This was the prevailing conceptualization of nation-state sovereignty. In the crafting of the Treaty on Conventional Forces in Europe (CFE) and pre-cursors of the E.U., European nations came to recognize that they could best protect their own security through mutual transparency and interdependence, thus the flowering of the macroregional community of the E.U.

When the dust settled after WWII, two superpowers emerged. No combination of other nations could counterbalance the capabilities of even one of them. Then, after 1991, there was only one, again with no obvious counterweight, though China's GDP has been steadily rising, and with it, its political influence.

Cooper does not call for dissolution of the conventional nation-state in his book. He asserts that, "the European Union is an organization not for pursuing a European interests, but for pursuing national interest more effectively. In the postmodern context 'more effectively' means without being obliged to resort to military means." Cooper thus seems to concur with former U.N. Secretary General Kofi Annan (2000/2004, 240-243), who has said that by no means is the Nation-State defunct but rather the "sovereign State" is a crucial tool to shield people from the upheavals of globalization.

My philosophy professor used to say, "Your rights stop where my nose begins." Similarly, Solana, Cooper, and Annan all recognize the value of sovereignty, as long as sovereignty of a given nation-state does not bruise the noses of the other nation-states because the resulting brawl can become intercontinental.

Cooper calls the members of the E.U.—and other countries moving toward cooperation and big-picture policies, such as Japan—"postmodern" nations. During this epoch of openings and mutuality, he points out that the U.S. and China remain stubbornly "modern."[48] Even Zbigniew Brzezinski (2007), largely considered a hawk during his tenure in the Carter administration, has criticized American foreign policy as selfish, arbitrary, and narrow. In pursuit of short-term fixes, the U.S. has resorted to military force, which is itself expensive (Stiglitz estimated the cost of the Iraq war at $3 trillion) and may be even more expensive in social and economic costs in the long-term.

An-Na'im (2008) consistently frames his argument for the dominance of the secular nation-state over "sovereignty" of the Islamic community because he points out that the nation-state allows for religious practice, but theocracies do not allow for anything but their own program.

Acknowledging that the word "sovereignty" is used to advance particular agendas in particular scenarios, Michael Ignatieff offers a thoughtful approach to sovereignty in the context of the questions of human rights violations. He notes that the report of the International Commission on State Sovereignty defined only two instances of human rights abuse that justified violating nation-state sovereignty: "apprehended genocidal massacre or massive ethnic cleansing." Ignatieff adds, "Significantly, the report did not believe coercive military force was justifiable in the case of tyranny involving serial forms of human rights abuse the level of massacre or ethnic cleansing." What Ignatieff does not explicitly say, but which may be behind his analysis, is that more respect for the sovereignty of struggling and impoverished countries may be necessary, an approach used by George Mitchell, who

---

[48] Cooper's (2003) word, for which I substitute "narrow".

brokered peace in Northern Ireland, and Richard Holbrooke, engineer of peace among the leaders of Bosnia, Serbia, and Croatia in Dayton in 1995. In the vein of Taylor (1994), what needed to happen for the sub-groups coming to the table was that they needed to be "seen" to as great an extent as making material reparations and planning future power-sharing arrangements.

What I am suggesting, given sovereignty's evolution from a term that did not even have political connotations in the late Middle Ages and Renaissance to a concept now swollen to nearly absolute, reckless self-determination, is *negotiated sovereignty*. I believe the world must undertake a conversion to sovereignty that entails reciprocity, mutuality, and transparency—one very much based on how Robert Cooper (2003) sees the nation-state maturing from a polity that is narrowly self-interested to one that is strengthened and protected by strengthening and protecting its neighbors. One could argue that this is precisely what the United States has been doing since 1941, but this trend was dangerously reversed after September 11, 2001, as discussed by Brzezinski (2005a, 2005b, 2007a, 2007b, 2008), Ignatieff (2003, 2004a, 2005a, 2005c, 2007) and others.

Though they understand the need to use "sovereignty" in the Westphalian sense, to reassure other nation-states of American resolve not to interfere with them, President Obama and Secretary of State Hillary Rodham Clinton have also acknowledged the effect of U.S. actions in a more global way, rather than the outdated, narrow attention to American interests.

Secretary of State Clinton has expressed an awareness of the U.S. as one nation-state in a larger system—and has acknowledged that the U.S. must "modernize and revitalize" international organizations and create new global governing institutions. In Berlin, Candidate Obama declared himself to be a "citizen of the world" and again focused on international mutual acknowledgment and benefits in his speech in Strasbourg (2009b).

# CHAPTER EIGHT. THE COMFORT OF A SHELL

What crosses boundaries? Defining globalization. An "Aterritorial" world? Synergy of sovereignty and boundedness. The vertebrate-cellular analogy. Interdependence in an unbounded world. Entangled Universalisms. Selecting boundaries.

\*

The story of mass migrations (voluntary and forced) is hardly a new feature of human history. But when it is juxtaposed with the rapid flow of mass-mediated images, scripts, and sensations, we have a new order of instability in the production of modern subjectivities. As Turkish guest workers in Germany watch Turkish films in their German flats, as Koreans in Philadelphia watch the 1988 Olympics in Seoul through satellite feeds from Korea, and as Pakistani cabdrivers in Chicago listen to cassettes of sermons recorded in mosques in Pakistan or Iran, we see moving images meet denationalized viewers. These create diasporic public spheres, phenomena that confound theories that depend on the continued salience of the nation-state as the key arbiter of important social changes.

—Arjun Appadurai, *Modernity at Large: Cultural Dimensions of Globalization* (1996a, 4).

Sovereignty, boundedness, and unity—three of the four properties that I claim should be rethought—all run deep in the popular conception of the nation-state. People do not like being reminded that President Woodrow Wilson carved up Eastern Europe to match his primordialist view of ethnic groups, or that the Middle East was dissected by Great Britain largely for imperial convenience. Something as big as the nation-state seems to sit much more comfortably if we can convince ourselves that its outline is ancient and immutable. Jürgen Habermas comments on this discomfort, connecting the ideas of boundedness and unity. He says, "This is why recourse to a nation with organic roots is able to conceal the contingency of what have happened to become state borders. Nationalism confers on these borders, an aura of imitated substance and inherited legitimacy. The naturalized nation can thus symbolically fasten and fortify the territorial and social integrity of the nation-state." (1996, 288)

Nation-states were initially imagined to have clear boundaries that the government could maintain. People and other living things, commodities, and abstractions—including money and ideas—now cross those boundaries at an unprecedented speed and volume. In addition to explicit geopolitical nation-state borders, boundaries have included distances, frontiers, fences, gates, laws, membranes, oceans, firewalls, outlines, passwords, portals, skins, shells, taboos, or other hindrances or checkpoints—both abstract and actual—that stopped some things at the door while letting others through.

Boundedness is more than the sovereignty and protection of citizens. That boundaries are dissolving is an artifact of modernity—begun in the Renaissance, Enlightenment and Industrial Revolution. Nation-state *un*boundedness continues in the 21st century via what some call *hyper*-globalization. *Whole Earth Catalog* editor Stewart Brand is credited with the expression "information wants to be free." Money and people want to be free too—to flow where they choose, not to be constrained by governments and other impediments. Therefore, as the combined revolutions of freedom, individuality, instantaneous communications and other technologies have allowed those flows, they have seeped into places they could never reach before.

How boundaries have been re-defined affects how people see nation-state unity in its several meanings, as well as how they see achingly significant concepts like identity and home. This chapter argues that although the metaphorical "shell" of nation-state seems comforting, the "shell" will be and *should* be made more porous if the nation-state is to survive and thrive.

## Defining Globalization

I began this discussion by defining boundaries and boundedness as they were conceived early in the evolution of the nation-state, but the fact is that diminishing sovereignty, global capitalism, multiculturalism, and globalization—the current reality—also concern *un*boundedness.

The porousness of previously fortified and controllable nation-state boundaries is the result of the amplified globalization that Appadurai (1996a) aptly describes above. Globalization is the opposite of the boundedness of nation-states as originally conceived. When I teach about globalization, the definition I give for this vast and multifaceted phenomenon is the following: Globalization is the term used for increased interdependence and integration since the 1980s—culturally and economically, most markedly through trade, finance, and communication technologies. : Globalization refers to four types of increased flows: money, resources, ideas, and people. These flows lead to maximization of profit through efficiency, vast wealth creation, greater impoverishment in raw numbers, cross-cultural exposure, and the insecurity and radicalization.

Globalization has been driven by ever-cheaper and faster transportation and communications that enable the flow of investments, revenues, finished goods, raw materials, personal messages, and cultural products (including films, music, and even video statements by Osama bin Laden), as well as the movement of human beings across nation-state boundaries. Globalization has also been described as a "complex connectivity" (Tomlinson 1999) producing new patterns of behavior and meaning, as social ties can be formed and maintained across previously impractical distances.

The world gets "smaller" when ideas, money, and cause and effect can leap its physical distances with fewer resources expended. The globe has been swelling and shrinking since the age of the Greeks and Romans, whose seafaring trade and systems of roads "globalized" the banks of the Mediterranean Sea, the European continent, and the tip of Africa. Other historically significant globalizing events included the first Muslim attacks on Constantinople in 674 and 699 A.D., Marco Polo's journey with his uncle and father to the Mongol Empire and China in the late 13th century, British colonialism, instantaneous communication via telegraphy beginning in the 1840s, and World Wars I and II, during which many combatants first came into contact with people from foreign lands. Soldiers from neighborhoods in the Bronx and the farms of Iowa fought side-by-side, suddenly regarding themselves as fellow Americans in a larger world. Whereas previously they may have identified themselves primarily in regional terms, they now placed themselves for the first time as inhabitants of a larger *globe*; this shift in thinking happened on a mass scale during the two world wars.

In other periods, by contrast, the distances between people became insurmountable, with instability and danger in the hinterlands between metropolises. *De*-globalizing events have included the Fall of Rome and ensuing shut-down of trade routes for a millennium and the erection of the Berlin Wall, whose purpose was to stop the flow of people, goods, money, and messages between the Capitalist and Communist worlds.

Unlike other waves of social change because of interconnections and interdependence of world players, the globalization of today stands in contrast to every other era of intense globalization (during the Roman Empire, the first wave of the industrial revolution, the economic booms before and after WWI, etc.) in that the most recent globalization works in direct opposition to the dominant institution of the time, because people can and want to maintain stronger alliances to their cultural sub-groups than to the nation-state.

## An "Aterritorial" World?

Has globalization begun to "denationalize" the world? Scholarly and public writing of the 1990s began to use a new word, "aterritorial." Physical barriers to human movement had fallen, and new highways for the movement of information, money and resources were being made ever-more accessible. The old assumption on which the sovereignty of the nation-state was based was being challenged because raw materials could be mined in one place, refined in another, assembled in yet a third, and ultimately consumed up to twelve thousand miles away. The ancient yearnings of profiteers, explorers, and travelers to locate a sea route to India from Europe, to carve a canal through Panama, to hurtle steel rails across continents, or dispatch telegraphs at the speed of thought were being realized in ways even Jules Verne and H.G. Wells could not have imagined.

The Iron Curtain had been pulled aside and technology was opening the world. It suddenly seemed that distance was barely an impediment—that people could live where they wished, work where they wished, and obtain vanilla from Madagascar or salmon from the Bering Sea as easily as bread from the local bakery.

Both public and scholarly language from the 1990s anticipates the diminishing importance of geospace in response to the sheer volume and acceleration of people, resources, and information streaming through the world. This was seen as a remarkable and potentially scary development. Nation-states were the big glue that held things together, and they had been largely based on land, territory, space, and boundaries. Writers wondered: what will happen now that nation-states can no longer control what massive multinational corporations do, or where people migrate, or how microbes travel?

The erosion of nation-state boundaries had deeply personal implications too. People learn a language and grow into an identity in one place, then move to another for work. Their location might change, but their allegiances typically do not. How would this affect the functioning of the nation-state that had selected symbols, flags, emotionally weighty words, and pledges that school children recited for the purpose of keeping them loyal to a given nation-state? How would this shake the world-view of people who believe themselves to be *of* a particular nation-state? What does it mean for their sense of home, meaning, tradition, and the good life?

## Synergy of Sovereignty and Boundedness

Sovereignty is the *prima facie* property of the nation-state. The word appears nearly daily in political dialogue and other media—verbatim *as* "sovereignty." In contrast, boundedness and unboundedness are called by many names. Some degree of boundedness is necessary for the enforcement of sovereignty; nation-states and other entities need identifiable borders for "sovereignty" or self-determination to mean anything. The point of this discussion is that "sovereignty" has meant a great many things over the past several centuries. Given the emphasis on political scientist on the Peace of Westphalia, political sovereignty first meant no outside interference in domestic (initially choice of religious faith) matters of a given polity. "Sovereignty" quickly came to mean a nation-state's right to not be subject to a "flow" of *military* force across its national borders. Nation-states are *not supposed to* enter into other nation-states militarily—in terms of the historical documents, philosophical examination of sovereignty and public writings I have reviewed. To a lesser extent, sovereignty refers to the ability to refuse demands for taxes and other payments to outside political entities. Nations also typically maintain a monopoly on the right to initiate force against the citizenry within their boundaries. In the Weberian conception of the nation-state the idea of sovereignty and boundedness underlie his assertion that the state retains the right to initiate force within its borders.

Nation-state boundedness conceptually extends beyond this synergy of sovereignty and boundaries. Boundedness—or rather unboundedness—entails the flow of *everything other than state-sanctioned military force*: people and other living things, disease vectors, ideologies, raw materials, other commodities, illegal weapons, investment, funding for terrorists, purchase orders, goods and the receipts for those goods, movies, music, *pirated* movies and music, pictures, and emails and "Tweets" of a woman bleeding to death on the streets of Iran—none of which nation-states are much able to control anymore, whether or not they are members of the G8. It's not surprising that political scientists and other writers have discussed the changes in nation-state boundedness with a panicked tone. If the nation-state is a political body, then the analogy to our physical bodies is rather alarming. When we human beings can no longer control the outflow of *good* things (blood, air in our lungs, the contents of our stomachs or minds) or influx of *bad* things (microbes or poisons) into our bodies, it means humiliation or even death.

## The Vertebrate-Cellular Analogy

Arjun Appadurai builds on his own earlier work on globalization (1996a, 1996b) and the work of two other theorists of globalization,

Saskia Sassen (1991, 1994, 1996a, 1998, 2006) and Gayatri Chakravorty Spivak (1988, 1992, 1998, 1999), in a new study of one of its most disturbing dimensions—ethnicized conflict.

Appadurai advances a biological metaphor of globalization that characterizes the social structures of nation-states in an international state system as "vertebrate" or "vertebral" and non-state political movements and illicit financial flows as "cellular." (2006: 21, 25) Under Appadurai's theory, the former are hierarchical, rigid, and have "backbones" of communication, transportation, and rules that rely on the reciprocity and mutuality of the players in the system (e.g., nation-states, other signatories of agreements, political allies, financial institutions, and trading partners). The latter are transnationally dispersed non-state financial entities, such as diamond or gun merchants, political separatists, or non-state networks. These black and gray marketers and political movements are dependent on but tend to work around or outside of the vertebrate infrastructure and rules.

The obvious extension of the metaphor is that of a host and parasite, with the vertebrate social structures being the host and the cellular entities being the parasites. Appadurai doesn't use the word "parasite" once in his book. Still, the question is implied by his term "vertebral": have nation-states become unwitting hosts to parasitic non-states? By definition, actual parasites—such as the Ebola virus, mistletoe, or intestinal worms—have evolved in such a way that they do not usually kill their hosts quickly. Symbiotic relationships between some hosts and colonic flora have actually become necessary for the health of the host. Will some comparable evolution happen to the deprived, enraged and lawless actors of the political so they sap less of the life energy of the larger "organism"? Do they perhaps perform functions that are necessary for the health and welfare of the "vertebral" entities, but are in some way impractical for the "vertebral" entities to perform themselves?

## Interdependence

The subprime mortgage crisis of 2008 and ensuing economic downturn have revealed the interdependence of nation-states. Perhaps the most important dimension of what we now call "globalization" is the set of mutualities and interactions among the people and political entities of Planet Earth.

Connectedness or interdependence is the opposite walling oneself off or withdrawing into a shell. From a standpoint of national security, interdependence means being affected by extremism, bellicosity, cultural patterns, technological capabilities or economic patterns in countries beyond one's borders. In part because of the splash-over of such phenomena, the prerogative to intervene and stabilize or minimize threats to one's own country has been asserted by Cooper (2006b), Shultz (1985, 2006, 2007b) and Brzezinski (2007a, 2008). Among these writers and others touting preemptive self-preservation there is a sense that the national boundaries behind which people were able to feel secure have changed.

Brzezinski says, "We have to face the fact that the global system as it now exists was shaped largely between 1945 and 1950, when there were entirely different power realities. So the first order of business is to adjust the existing global institutions to these realities. Plus the reality that in the background are these volatile, restless, politically awakened masses that continue to put more and more pressure on the system...the possibility of diversified conflicts spurting all over the place the way sometimes a forest fire spreads and then leaps over boundaries because of winds." (2008, 28)

The concern Brzezinski raises supports the suggestion I make at the end of chapter nine: while the nation-state should be retained, the metanational or "global" institutions that regulate and coordinate them must be revamped and strengthened.

Although it brings new challenges, the newly-realized global connectedness also offers some hopeful possibilities. Theorist Marshall McLuhan once admonished, "There are no passengers on spaceship Earth. We are all crew..." (1964, 80) Our interconnectedness in ensuring that our planet will remain viable has been expressed by Kofi Annan (2003) and—as a mass epiphany—by former Vice President Al Gore in the quotation at the beginning of chapter two. In a more scholarly way, Martin Albrow (1996) expressed this same idea by predicting that planetary interdependence would become the most salient factor in international relations.

In spite of the analogy, unboundedness is not all bad for political bodies. Trade enriches traders and their societies on both sides of the transaction. Imagine one person with two fishing poles and another with two fishing hooks. If they trade so that each then has a hook and pole, wealth is actually *created*. This is one of the most primitive but illuminating demonstrations of the creation of wealth. It is not that the law of conservation of mass and energy has been broken, but by moving items to a state of superior utilization, each trader is enriched by the transaction. When the trade routes of Rome shut down after the fall of the empire in 476 AD, the entire Western world got poorer because it was no longer safe to travel the roads and trade metals, technologies, art, and ideas. Mercantile exchange of "good" things (enabled by the increasing unbounded of nation-states) makes the world more prosperous.

In chapter two, I quoted Thomas Friedman on the fall of the Berlin Wall. The most important change was not the elimination of the physical wall, but the end of the barrier to people's ability to share and process information. There are magnificent and empowering dimensions to having nearly instantaneous access to millions of pages of books, thousands of films, breaking news and electronic letters from friends. At the same time, the volume and relentlessness of information can be psychologically overwhelming. The freedom to see some images, engage in some conversations, purchase some products, and have a range of vicarious experiences can be intoxicating for people who would have been constrained and protected by social norms and technological limitations in previous eras.

## Entangled Universalisms

The erosion of boundaries forces symbiosis of things that once were separate. With the wave of globalization that accompanied the Industrial Revolution, people were forced to contend with other cultures alien to their own. The cognitive response was to seek larger rules sets that explained alien norms and perspectives more universally.

This understandable urge to simplify the template for social reality can lead to gross misunderstandings as people from one culture encounter outsiders. One example is the way in which the monotheistic, transcendent religion that people practiced in Europe was not really analogous to the spiritual practice of the Japanese or Chinese or Asian Indians, as Spickard (2007) points out. Nonetheless, Eastern spiritual practice was crammed under the heading of "religion." Combined with the power dynamic of colonizers taking control of other societies, this led to a nearly irresistible urge for the (comparatively recent) values of modernity—individualism, efficiency, precedence of logic over intuition, short-term maximization of utility, etc. to be touted as *the* (universally applicable) truth rather than *a* truth of one portion of the world. [49]

In his long discussion of the mistake of envisioning the nation-state as ethnically pure (which I discuss further in chapter nine), Arjun Ap-

---

[49] Keeping in mind that the "the truth" vs. "an idea" distinction is not linguistically possible in all languages.

padurai talks about the "universalisms" of the free market, freedom, individualism, democracy, and human rights. First, each of these competes with others from the list, necessitating negotiation. Second, universalisms, often described as absolute, are in practice anything but that. The free market is not truly free, but a complex morass of privileges for the already privileged lain over a supposedly level field of market exchanges. How this plays out in metanational organizations like the W.T.O. and World Bank is the subject of Joseph Stiglitz's *Globalization and Its Discontents* (2002), and how to correct ways in which such financial arrangements keep the poor of the world poor is the subject of *Making Globalization Work* (2006). Increased freedom to act without social punishment was clearly one of the positive outcomes of the Renaissance, but freedom to consume the planet's resources until it is shriveled husk is a freedom that benefits no one in the long-term. Similarly, individualism that depletes the common good is not desirable, but how is this to be reframed, if unregulated self-enrichment has been touted as an absolute right? Zakaria (2003) is one of the most trenchant critics of the universalism of democracy, pointing out that, if people are rushed into democracy without a well-crafted constitution and a popular culture to protect minorities, the result will be "illiberal democracy"—mob rule of the majority. In chapter seven, I discussed one of the major problems with the universalism of human rights—it polarizes competing factions as perpetrator and victim.

Each of these universalisms has taken on the quality of an inviolable, absolutely applicable rule, but simultaneously comes into conflict with others from the list. The only way to craft a workable situation is to back off of the absolutism in which these principles were conceived, since one cannot negotiate the absolute.

145

# The Comfort of a Shell

Growing up in the Pennsylvania countryside, I would sometimes turn over a rock to see centipedes scurry away or newts burrow in, and I would sometimes pick up what we called a "pill bug" to see it curl into a tightly plated ball. These terrestrial crustaceans are named *Armadillidium vulgare*. This scientific label refers to another animal with armor to protect itself—the armadillo. The pill bug or wood louse has extremely sensitive antennae; it can feel the tiniest vibrations and will stay closed until the threat is gone. As I held them in my hand, I wondered what it would do if didn't release it, allowing it to emerge and crawl away safely. Would it starve? Could it get stuck inside its shell? My point is that there is such a thing as an excessively effective shell.

Boundaries are the protection for a nation-state—its shell, if you will. The dominant social structures have not always had hard shells. While the oldest cities, like Jericho, *did* have walls to keep marauders out, empires—whether Roman, Mongolian, or Persian—took on an entirely different topology. They functioned from centers of control with tentacles of influence, rather than having nonporous and strictly defined boundaries.

Boundedness was a useful concept for the emergent nation-state because it addressed the problem of conflicting authorities. However, in a world of mixing money, good, culture and labor forces, the watertight nation, in An-Na'im's (2002) turn of phrase, will become stagnant.

Another way to consider boundaries and the nation-state is to consider how dysfunctional utopian governments have historically been: they have striven to seal themselves off from the world and have pursued increasingly brutal measures to keep people, products, currency or cultural influences on one side or the other of a wall. Interestingly, Brzezinski (1970) predicted two decades before the fall of the Soviet

146

Union that its inability to respond to an increasingly technological globalization would lead to far-reaching instability there and in Eastern Europe. He turned out to be right.

To this analysis of boundaries and the growing unboundedness of the nation-state, Habermas adds the following: "Globalization signifies transgression, the removal of boundaries and thus a danger for a nation-state which almost neurotically watches its borders." (1996, 291) Habermas' choice of the pejorative yet insightful "neurotically" suggests agreement that the goal of absolutely impermeable boundaries is not desirable (even if it were attainable).

The power of nation-states has historically been power over land from which resources come and on which people reside. National borders or boundaries are simultaneously actual barriers to territory outside the nation-state and all of the associated symbolic and legal representations of "boundary." The boundedness of the nation-state has meant that the government has the power (1) to assert that—and where—a line exists, and (2) to use force to stop things from moving across that line.

A useful exercise in rethinking nation-state boundedness might be to concentrate less on the borders and more on the things that now move across them: specifically, whether they are beneficial or toxic in the effects of their movement. For example, control over flows of transnational workers is Pyrrhic at best—and at worst, truly destructive of the spirit of a republic. It encourages racialized resentment by justifying the xenophobia of supposedly ancestral citizens who happened to get through the door a little sooner.

The reaction to concerns about the H1N1 flu virus in early 2009 offer some hope for moving in the right direction in this area. Experts worldwide agreed that it would be too oppressive to control the movement of everyone needing to travel internationally, but people were encouraged to be aware that they could be transmitting a disease. At Kansai and Narita international airports in Japan, thermographic imaging was used to check the body temperatures of passengers coming from Mexico to detect fevers that might be caused by flu infection. (Nonviolent) scrutiny of truly dangerous crossings may become increasingly appropriate.

By contrast, legalizing and then regulating and taxing the crossings of currently uncontrollable substances, such as marijuana, is a waste of resources, as well as being untenable in terms of any substantive harm that such criminalized substances cause.

Governmental spokespeople and those fighting culture wars make the argument that illicit drug consumption is a vice and intrinsically socially destructive. However, the American (and other nation-states) have legalized *other* vices (prostitution, alcohol consumption, gambling) where it has served their purposes (usually the enrichment of State coffers) to relinquish puritanical intrusion into private naughtiness. The more persuasive argument to me is that it would consume fewer governmental resources to legalize and regulate vices (including drugs) than is currently spent blocking their flow across nation-state boundaries—and the social outcomes would be better too, if resources could be channeled into treatment rather than interdiction and punishment.

The 21st century will require all nation-states and metanational entities to collectively, constructively identify those parts of traditional national boundedness that need to be maintained, those that need to be discarded wholesale, and those that need to change to keep up with the changes in the material world.

Attempts to stop the flow of information and ideas are futile, and will waste the resources and credibility of nations that try. Continued attempts to forbid consumer entertainment items such as movies, books, recreational drugs, and is futile, and will result in massive waste, destruction of essential liberties, and (most destructively of all) corruption of law enforcement. Nation-states must acknowledge the immorality and futility of keeping workers that an economy needs away from jobs that the workers need, based upon the accident of birth location or politico-historical frontiers. Socially imagined characteristics such as ethnicity[50] must be expunged from statutes, while recognition of cultural and value differences is retained.

Nation-states must increase cooperation and work harder to control and report on the spread of infectious disease. They must acknowledge that corruption and lawlessness within their borders will absolutely affect people outside their borders—and they must define protocols by which the global polity can protect itself from bad actors—regardless of which imaginary lines in the sand they attempt to hide behind. The entire planet is affected by pollution and destruction of resources, and we need ways to address these issues. The upside of the Westphalian nation-state was that its creation—including its sovereignty—brought an end to the never-ending post-Renaissance wars in Europe. Sadly, the solution to one problem created another: it now sometimes seems as if the only way to resolve international conflict is through violence or the threat of violence. It is time for us to separate the wheat from the chaff: to keep the good that came from the Westphalian treaties and to replace that which no longer works.

---

[50] Ethnicity is more imaginary than it is biological. We can tell this is true because being a "gypsy" (Romani) matters in Hungary or Romania, while it scarcely matters beyond Eastern Europe. Ancestral caste status may matter to Indians living in the subcontinent while the trappings of that membership are invisible to others.

# CHAPTER NINE. UNITY LOOKING FORWARD OR LOOKING BACK

Placing the nation-state in social time. Purity as impetus for murder. Globalization accelerates backward-looking nation-state "unity." The will of a people. Unity in opposition. Looking up at the moon. Unity of purpose.

\*

This double code is revealed by the inscriptions of the collective memory: political milestones in the fight for civil rights join together with the military ceremonies in memory of soldiers killed in action. Both these traces mirror the ambiguous meaning of 'the nation'—the voluntary nation of citizens, who generate democratic legitimation, and inherited or ascribed nation of those, born into it, facilitating social integration. *Staatsbürger* or citizens are supposed to constitute themselves as an association for free and equal persons by choice; *Volksgenossen* or nationals *find* themselves formed by an inherited form of life and the fateful experience of a shared history. Built into the self-understanding of the national state, there is this tension between the universalism of an egalitarian community and the particularism of a cultural community bound together by origin and fate.

—Jürgen Habermas, Mapping the Nation (1996, 287).

Time is one of the most puzzling and painful entries in the human lexicon of ideas. Shared destiny and origin are the two dimensions of time that compete in our conception of the "unity" of the nation-state; we must always choose whether to look forward or backward. The Danish philosopher Kierkegaard (1844/1957, 38, 40, 55) explains that it is our very ability to conceive of time that fills us with anxiety. We remember the past; we act in the present, but we have desires about the future—which hasn't happened yet. Therefore we are filled with thoughts of something unreal, something that is—nothing.

Such questions of the meaning of the past and how to prepare for the future create agitation—trepidation in some and anger in others. Kierkegaard (1943) called this pit in the stomach "angst," and prescribed Protestant faith, obedience, and a sort of mysticism about the perfection of the divine.

Certainly, there are parallels that can be drawn between Kierkegaard's era of almost unbearable change and the late 20th/early 21st century. Appadurai's equivalent term for the unknown is "uncertainty," and it is a major theme of his work on globalization. The uncertainty of globalization makes it imperative for us to address the problem of nation-state unity soon or suffer devastating consequences.

## Placing the Nation-State in Social Time

Just as the concept of time complicates consciousness, so it complicates the social construction of the nation-state. A nation-state is necessarily built on a past, some set of traditions, family histories, and the concerted efforts of the people who founded it and first inhabited it, followed by its struggles, its current state of affairs—all based on and informing ideas about its destiny.

We can hear the word "unity" and related concepts in contemporary discourse on the nation-state. Jürgen Habermas and Arjun Appadurai are the thinkers who have most thoroughly unpacked the contradictions inherent in the idea of nation-state unity.

The expected property of "unity" is the central problem that the nation-state—or rather we, imagining it—must solve. The concept of unity may be expressed as "unified," "united," "union," society as a "whole," "community," "communion," "collective," "collectivity," "solidarity," or "integration." Regardless, I have found the linguistic pointers almost always fall into one of two categories: they either point backward to a soft-focus time of authenticity and integrity or forward to ideals of the nation-state.

Nowhere is this problem revealed with more searing clarity than by Jürgen Habermas in his chapter entitled "The European Nation-state—Its Achievements and Its Limits. On the Past and Future of Sovereignty and Citizenship" (1996). The quotation with which I began this chapter goes to the heart of the dilemma—literally, two ideas that are, in this case, in direct contradiction with one another. The first idea of the union of the nation-state can be found in France's motto: "liberté, égalité, fraternité." A nation-state whose nonreligious authority is legitimated (optimally) through even-handed treatment of the plebiscite and its needs, and whose sisterhood and brotherhood occurs through participation in a just state, not through a homogeneous cultural identity. France, and particularly Paris, had already experienced some globalization by 1789 and certainly by the post-Napoleonic era when the motto was formally adopted. The emphasis, even in the mythic dimension of the construction of one of the first nation-states, was a secular government that would attempt to smooth out some of the inequality between rich and poor.

This chronologically earlier meaning of the union of the nation-state is also embodied in the American Constitution and was urgently expressed by Abraham Lincoln through 20 uses of the word "union" in his 1861 inaugural speech and through his reference to the "unfinished work" of a "government of the people, by the people, for the people" in the Gettysburg Address. It's true that, in his inaugural speech, Lincoln mixed his message of a forward-looking unity of purpose with a backward-looking invocation of the "[t]he mystic chords of memory" of slain soldiers and early resolve to bolster the bonds of a nation-state that was on the verge of being nearly split asunder. This invocation is consistent with what Habermas sees as the necessary use of backward looking, i.e., cultural, bonds. Habermas (1996) says, "Without this cultural interpretation of political membership rights, the European national state in its initial period hardly would have had the strength to reach what I have described as its main achievement: namely, to establish a new, more abstract level of social integration in terms of the legal implementation of democratic citizenship."

## Purity as Impetus for Murder

The other crucial text on the problems of the imagined "unity" of the nation-state is Arjun Appadurai's book-length essay, *Fear of Small Numbers* (2006). More urgently voicing points made by Habermas, Appadurai also points to the mythos of ethnic purity embedded into some imaginings of the nation-state as its central flaw and landmine. He asks:

> Why should a decade dominated by a global endorsement of open markets, free flow of finance capital, and liberal ideas of constitutional rule, good governance, and active expansion of human rights have produced such a plethora of examples of ethnic cleansing on one hand and extreme forms of political violence against civilian populations (a fair definition of terrorism as a tactic) on the other?

His answer to the question is an extended metaphor of the nation-state as a "vertebrate" form of social organization. However, with the new capabilities of travel and communication, the globalized world also affords greater movement to "cellular" social organizations. In sum, globalization has increased the urgency with which claims of ancestral prerogative are asserted, while competing for the resources of the nation-state and global economy.

## Globalization Accelerates Backward-Looking Nation-State "Unity"

At this historical moment of global financial panic and upheaval in social structures, what we knew before has been disrupted. There are new capacities for everyone. There are victims in the race for profit. There is rule-breaking, or norms that have not been codified yet. Work, home, and self seem to be perpetually shifting sands. Globalization throws into question everything that previously seemed solid—macro social structures, identity, a sense of one's place in the world, and the confluence of nation and national culture, of nation and economy.

Appadurai cites this "uncertainty" caused by globalization as the root cause of frantic and violent ethnic or religious self-identification and persecution of "other." Globalization causes mixing of people, with people who consider themselves "natives" or "national" now competing for prizes both in the private market place and from a government that redistributes resources. Michael Ignatieff (1993, 2004b) has also explored the fuse of identity in a world of jostling, elbowing people from a variety of backgrounds.

No longer a solid set of givens, national identity is constructed as one of many flexible, fluid, potentially contradictory, negotiated identities flowing from language, birthplace, geospatial residence, education, profession, religion, leisure, comparative privilege or deprivation, and even Internet-based social networks, such as Facebook or My Space. It is the emotional and what Charles Taylor calls "anguished" search for identity, recognition, and perpetuation of one's culture that has driven some of the tribalism and violence of the past two decades. Taylor (1994) traced the origins of acknowledgement, respect, and standing in society, and concluded with the warning that particularity-blind proceduralism is too biased toward Western culture. More recently, Taylor (2004) looked for "multiple modernities"—varied conceptions of power-sharing and resource allocation under the aegis of the nation-state.

## The Will of a People

An early idea of unity, dating to Enlightenment thinkers, maintains that the people of the nation *collectively consent* to be part of the nation-state. This persuasive idea can be seen in numerous American and French documents. Because the American and French Revolutions played such a dramatic role in late 18th century embodiment and conceptualization of the nation-state, these ideas of what the nation-state is and how it is "unified" have spread in the way people talk about the nation-state and the way it is put into social practice. We need to take very seriously the way in which mottos, images, words, and metaphors reflect how the nation-state is imagined: the words we use create the reality we occupy.

The French philosopher Ernest Renan wrote an essay, "Qu'est-ce qu'une nation?"[51] a little more than a century after the French Revolution. Responding to the essay's title question, Renan wrote memorably that a nation is defined by the "daily" and collective agreement of the people of the nation to participate in it. He expressed this in the phrase that "nation" was the manifestation of the people, "avoir fait de grandes choses ensemble, vouloir en faire encore" (having done great things together and wishing to do more). Renan's language perfectly captures the importance of considering how the nation-state is placed in time: Renan talks about looking backward to former accomplishments of a given nation-state, but he also suggests the importance of

---

[51] What is a nation?

155

looking forward, as we would all do if the nation-state were a sort of conveyance that we were riding and steering together.

Renan wrote his famous essay during the dispute over the Alsace-Lorraine region between France and Germany. Other theorists[52] have since disagreed with Renan, but his essay is nonetheless considered a foundation of the conception of the nation-state.

Although the backward-looking interpretation of unity can be lethal as an impetus to ethnic hostilities, the forward-looking connotation of nation-state unity is crucial. As Habermas (1996, 285) asserts, "The constitutional state is conceived as a political order which is voluntarily established by the will of the people, so that the addressees of legal norms can at the same time understand themselves as the authors of the law." Habermas asserts that investing the modern, bureaucratic administration of privileges and protection with emotional weight was absolutely necessary to inspire citizens to get into the harness and pull together. He says, "The interpretation of the nation as prepolitical entity allows it to uphold an unchanged early modern image of external sovereignty that is but imbued with nation colours, as it were. This is the place where the secularized state preserves a residue of sacred transcendence...."

Consistent with Habermas' assessment, Benedict Anderson's renowned explanation of the early notion of a nation-state asserts that the mythology of belonging to a nation-state persuaded populations to cooperate with nation-states such as Thailand and other Southeastern Asian and South American countries that took the European nation-state as their model. Anderson says self-identification as citizens of a nation-state was accelerated through media artifacts such as maps

---

[52] For example, Smith and Hutchinson (1995, 1432-33) disputed Renan's assertion that people are consciously participating in what Renan called "a daily plebiscite".

showing nation-state boundaries, museums mythologizing a glorious history, and censuses categorizing people as "nationals."

As I explained in chapter seven, I believe that our use of language around the word "sovereignty" to promote the idea of a "will of the people" or even the "will of a nation" is meaningful, even useful, as long as the consensus of the majority leaves room for dissent. While "will" is something that people can choose; ethnicity is not.

## Unity Against

There is one other sense in which several authors I have reviewed here have used the word and concept of "unity:" In the sense of unity against a threat. Shultz, Brzezinski, and Barnett, (not surprisingly, the most militaristic in my group of 16 thinkers), have each talked about nations or citizens of a nation standing firm against threats such as communism or terrorism.

Barnett argues that developed countries should unify to "export se-curity" and smooth the transition to globalization and modernity for the "disconnected gap." Barnett (2004, 2005). He recommends doing this through waves of integration into existing macroregional al-liances, such as NATO and the E.U. Barnett also recommends that, if and when new members (such as Iraq) are added to the integrated core, they should be supported by the West. Barnett means this in a military sense, but I note that economically supporting new core members in the ways that Stiglitz has described (and as I discuss fur-ther in chapter ten) is crucial. Barnett also points out that America's Unified Command Plan, now consisting of four regional commands that encompass "gap" countries, will and should be reorganized. He says, "The current Unified Command Plan divides the world in bands running north to south, whereas the enemies we fight in this global war on terrorism tend to network more in an east-west fashion, thus confounding our efforts by creating a host of unwanted seams in which coordination tends to break down among the current regional commanders." (2005, 216)

Both Brzezinski (2005b) and Barnett (2005) warn against America "going it alone." A central concept in the work of Barnett (2004, 2005) is "connectedness," that is, awareness of and compliance with international social and political norms. China is at the fulcrum of Barnett's geographical analysis (2004) of the "integrated core" (politically and socially connected nation-states) and "the gap" (countries struggling with their own poverty and cultural ambivalence about the pressures and uncertainties of modernity).

In *The Pentagon's New Map* (2004), Barnett argues that (1) China is part of the core, since it craves financial benefit from the "old core" (the U.S., U.K., and Great Powers of Europe), and (2) preparation for war with China after the end of the Cold War was a grave tactical error. His failure to share others' enthusiasm for pumping up the military in preparation for a Sino-West confrontation may have played a role in costing Dr. Barnett his job at the Naval War College.

Yet in *Blueprint for Action* (2004) that followed *Pentagon's New Map*, Barnett was still wrestling with the problem of China. The historical nation-state once entailed a confluence of political power, cultural unity, and financial interests. In simple terms, economic globalization (which drives cultural and other globalization) has caused these elements of the nation and nation-state to pull apart. How then to get business concerns and countries like China with mushrooming economic power to adhere to and participate in the international community and conventions of human rights, environmental negotiations, security concerns, etc.? This question is related to the breakdown that Stiglitz identified and that I discussed in chapter five: the formal protections of the nation-state do not protect the most vulnerable people from the informal global economy. Barnett (2005, 156) puts it this way: "Simply put, China's political connectivity with the outside world has not kept pace with its economic connectivity, and its security connectivity is—quite frankly—virtually nonexistent compared with its growing technological connectivity. China takes from the world but does not yet know what it should give back to the larger community." Interestingly, this sounds similar to the awareness of interconnectedness and interdependence for which Habermas and Cooper advocate.

## The Problem of the "Unity" of the Nation-State

The solutions that I suggest lie in the placement of the nation-state in time.

The first solution suggested by Habermas to the problem of "unity" mirrors the separation of church and state that, like the nation-state itself, has roots in the resolution of the Thirty Year's War. I advocate separation of *culture* and state, and offer the following advice for legislators and executives of nation-states: *Do not try to make laws about what culture is accepted or mainstream or morally attractive or repugnant.* In doing so, you reinforce the primacy of the ancestral or majoritarian nation and propagate a mistake in the original conception of the nation-state—that each one has an essential or "first" religion, race, or cultural template that can legitimately be used to condone acts ranging from exclusion to outright extermination of the *"other,"* the newcomers, outsiders, or deviants by virtue of skin color, faith or habit.

The second solution suggested by Habermas is a reformed and improved social safety net such as that implemented by European governments after WWII. He says, "My suspicion is that a liberal political culture can hold together multicultural societies only if democratic citizenship pays in terms not only of liberal and political rights, but of

159

social and cultural rights as well." (1996, 290) By this he is specifically referring to collectivizing some resources, such as money for school, a social safety and other common goods. He adds, "Democratic citizenship develops its force of social integration, that is to say it generates solidarity between strangers, if it can be recognized and appreciated as the very mechanism by which the legal and material infrastructure of actually preferred forms of life is secured." And in this sentence is an echo of *The Needs of Strangers* (1984), Ignatieff's meditation on the material well-being of people in a society who must envision some sense of the other people with whom they share a city or a country.

While the other terms (sovereignty, boundedness, and modernity) that I examine in chapters seven, eight, and ten have a variety of meanings, nation-state "unity" is a duality, defined by placing the social construction of the nation-state in time. Nation-state unity can mean unity of ethnicity, cultural norms, language or race, or a dominant majority. Or it can mean consensus, agreement, choice, volition, and participation or inclusion in a secularist, universalist, and procedurally oriented republic where a written body of law applies equally to all participants in the society.

The specific term "unity" is not always explicitly identified as the concept that the writer is exploring. The words "unity" or "unified" or "united" or "union" or "indivisible" can be heard most frequently in emotionally charged public language, such as political documents and speeches. Three of many examples occur in the Preamble to the U.S. Constitution, "in Order to form a more perfect Union," the fragile optimism of the Pledge of Allegiance first published 27 years after the Civil War nearly tore the country apart ("one nation"), and the motto "*e pluribus unum*" (out of many, one) found on the seal of the United States.

A third solution to the problem of the duality of "unity" is suggested—merely intimated—by Habermas, and it is related to the thinking of Robert Cooper (2003) and some other thinkers whose work I examine here, such as Kofi Annan. Habermas says, "This tension can be solved on the condition that the constitutional principles of human rights and democracy give priority to a cosmopolitan understanding of the nation as a nation of citizens over and against an ethnocentric interpretation of the nation as a prepolitical entity." Nearer to the end of his essay, he cites the need for a "'post-national' self-understanding of the constitutional state," by which he means not culturally nationalistic. He criticizes the unwillingness of the German Supreme Court to participate in further expansion of the E.U. on grounds that the constitutional state needs a more explicitly stated cultural identity. Habermas responds to this by saying, "This argument is symptomatic of a defensive attitude which in fact accelerates that erosion of citizenship [the court] intends to counter."

Cooper's (2003) corresponding point is that, after WWII but during the period of the most intense fears of exchange of nuclear weaponry, national governments in Europe found that, counter-intuitively, more shared governance and greater cooperation, erosion of boundaries, and cross-intrusion into internal affairs led to greater preservation of national security for E.U. members and other countries (e.g., Japan) that Cooper cites as "postmodern." (Although this view downplays the argument that this evolution was conducted under the U.S. security umbrella.)

Similarly, Kofi Annan has said that by no stretch of the imagination does he advocate the weakening of the nation-state structure, that in the framework of a cooperative system such as the U.N., nation-state governments are necessary to help shield their citizens from the upheaval of globalization.

## Looking up at the Moon

This book does not showcase images of planet Earth, as nearly every political text does today. Rather, the Moon might constitute a more apt symbol of both emotional and purposeful political unity. It was, ironically, in the race to the Moon that humankind rediscovered "unity," both in a national and larger sense. The Moon shot was a landmark of the race to perfect intercontinental ballistic missile delivery systems as much as it was a manifestation of President Kennedy's vision of American will. Yet in the ability to escape the Earth and visit another heavenly body, the rare forward-looking yet emotionally compelling event transpired.

Two editorials below put words to that rediscovery. Commenting on U.S.-Soviet cooperation, George Washington University professor of political science Chandra Agarwal wrote in the *New York Times*:

> The nations themselves are aware of this danger [of nuclear war], and even within the obsolete framework of the 'nation-state' system, countries yearn for such universal cooperation as will check the drift toward political disintegration and intensification of conflicts. (1968, 22).

And an unnamed *Times of India* contributor ("On the Moon," 1969) wrote in response to the Apollo 11 mission:

> The earth is a grain of sand on a limitless seashore. That knowledge is now reaffirmed and should point to the need, here on earth, for humility, tranquility and an urge towards brotherhood. Let us hope that those indelible footprints on the moon mark a new epoch of peace and goodwill.

These and other editorial texts from the time of the space race, and the quotation with which I begin this chapter, illustrate that photographs of the Earth—and a new symbolism for the only other heavenly body that human beings have yet visited—gave people a wake-up call, a new sense of the need for what I call forward-looking unity on Earth.

This resonates with what Cooper (2003) and Habermas (1996) call postmodern or postnational nationalism—care for one's own, but with the awareness of a wider world and interdependence.

The forward-looking destiny of any given nation-state includes idealistic dreams for justice and prosperity, and is seldom the impetus for mass murder. This might mean a programmatic vision for a secular and inclusive nation of immigrants, or it might mean inclusion—if not perfect consensus—in social and political decision-making.

In his speech in Strasbourg (2009b), President Obama furthered the work of envisioning and helping the public to envision postnational cooperation and interdependence. He deprecated selfish interests by saying, "No more will the world's financial players be able to make risky bets at the expense of ordinary people." One potent linguistic thread that emerged in his speech was the idea of the commons, which are ruined if everyone treats them carelessly. Obama, with his sophisticated mind, is probably aware of Garrett Hardin's famous essay, "The Tragedy of the Commons." In fact, the word "common" occurred in the 3,500-word speech 15 *times*, once as a synonym for "ordinary" and once as a synonym for "frequent." The other 13 times, Obama used the word to mean "shared" or "collective." This extraordinary emphasis suggests a promising re-imagining of unity.

Inclusion in political dialogue and shared forward-looking goals must be predicated on a shared picture of a good world—a better world— and navigational rules to set sail for that world. This is the re-imagining of nation-state unity that I recommend. Tranquility and prosperity can never be built upon old grudges, remembered pain and racist and vengeful "unity."

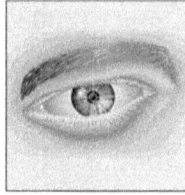

# CHAPTER TEN. FULFILLING THE PROMISE OF MODERNITY

A brief history of modernity. Informational, cognitive, and normative change. The difference between modernity and modernism. Modernity as a property of the nation-state. Suggested directions for modernity of the nation-state. The unfulfilled promise of modernity. Re-committing to lawfulness and consistency.

\*

[I]t behooves us to retrace the path of the philosophical discourse of modernity back to its starting point—in order to examine once again the directions once suggested at the chief crossroads. ...[T]he paradigm of the knowledge of objects has to be replaced by the paradigm of mutual understanding between subjects capable of speech and action.

—Jürgen Habermas, *The Philosophical Discourse of Modernity* (1987, 294-295).

Modernity is old news. As a social pattern, modernity has now been more than half a millennium in the making. The word came into the English language as many as *thirteen centuries ago* via the Latin adverb *modo* (meaning "recently" or "just now"). In English, it appears as an adjective, "modern," and a noun, "modernity."

Modernity is also old news in that the concepts and techniques that led to the spectacular productivity of the Industrial Revolution—among them logic, reliance on evidence, systemization, interchangeability, standardization, centralization, commoditization, and the privileging of private needs and private commerce over the common good—have lost their luster.

Our society now teeters on the brink of enormous change—a change perhaps unparalleled even by the Great Leap Forward[53] to using stone tools, the transition to agriculture, entry into the Gutenberg Galaxy,[54] the first instantaneous communication via telegraphy, or the global age as described by public figures from former Vice President Al Gore to political sociologist Martin Albrow.[55]

"Modernity" is used as code for capitalism, nationalism, globalization, and other exploitative political and social processes. It is not possible to understand where society might be going next without understanding modernity and retracing our steps, as Habermas suggests; it is not possible to understand modernity without grasping how people lived their lives and saw the world before the shift to modernity. Only from that base of understanding can we then discuss modernity as propagated by the nation-state—and how that modernity must reform and evolve.

---

[53] The term that Jared Diamond uses in *Guns, Germs and Steel* (1997) to probe pre-human development for clues to later differentials among the people of Africa, Eurasian, the Americas, and Pacifica. Also used in precisely the opposite sense as the unintentionally ironic sobriquet for Mao's program of forced resettlement from the city to the country.

[54] McLuhan (1962).

[55] Martin Albrow advances this thesis in his book, *The Global Age* (1996), contending that society is shifting out of modernity and into a new paradigm in which the object of analysis for society will be the planet itself—in all its fragility and vulnerability. However, no one makes this argument for a shift toward popular consideration of the planet as a whole as a political unit so powerfully as Al Gore. The former Vice President's documentary (David Guggenheim, 2006) on climate change shows a second iconic image of planet Earth, the "big blue marble" photograph taken on December 7, 1972 by the crew of Apollo 17, as further catalyst of the environmental movement that he claims was stimulated when the public saw the 1969 photograph, "Earthrise."

Thus this chapter begins by revisiting the historical origins of modernity. I then turn to the outmoded and destructive side of modernity, which I call "modernism," explore the symbiosis between modernity and the nation-state, and propose an overhaul of modernity in the nation-state, based on my analysis of texts by the thinkers listed in chapter three.

## A Brief History of Modernity

To understand modernity, it is necessary to evoke a picture of the *ancien regime*—the pre-industrial era when most of the population was rural, and power and wealth were entirely land-based. The economy was rooted neither in future harvests nor fiat currency, but in tangible livestock and crops from *this* season. The decline of the guild system in the late fourteenth century (which had peaked in the twelfth century) was a harbinger of the end of the economic and political system of feudalism. With the rise of mercantile port towns, guilds lost their exclusivity of trade. Guild dominance was subsumed by a market economy, which morphed into capitalism beginning in the late 18th century.

Money as is it now used and understood was barely in existence during the Middle Ages. First society had to convert from barter to the use of precious metal coins. Then the concept of indirect investment and the accrual of interest took centuries to emerge. Barter was sufficient for regions that were completely isolated from any place more than a day or two away on foot or horseback. Towns were largely self-sufficient in terms of food and other goods. People grew and made by hand what they needed and traded for what they could not grow or make; few pursued specialized professions. Almost everyone needed to know how to build a fire, milk a goat, or make a splint for a broken arm. There was no growth of the economy outside of military conquest, and people did not think in terms of their children attaining higher status or more prosperity than they had attained in their time.

Until modernity unfolded, people did the same work that their parents had done. Barring freak weather (which generally made things worse, not better), the same quantity of milk, wool, meat, hides, and grain was gathered each year.

Disease was rampant and its propagation mysterious. Factoring in infant mortality, life expectancy in England was about 36 years in 1800. The quality of life was miserable.

Though modernity is so vast and pervasive a shift that it is problematic to point to a particular technological catalyst, social scientists and theorists of mass communication often point to Johannes Gutenberg's development in the 1440s of the first alphabetic, movable metal-type printing press as the beginning of the Modern Age. This technology made information more widely accessible and affordable in the form of more books and pamphlets, and is generally considered the most momentous invention of the second millennium. In the 15th century, a hand-copied book cost approximately a month's pay; once they were mass-produced and less expensive, however, people could and did buy their own books. This trend started with bibles but later spread to other texts and periodicals.

## Informational, Cognitive, and Normative Change

The printing press catalyzed several radical cultural changes. Both modernity and the mass distribution of texts entail prioritization of *logos*—facts and demonstrable knowledge—over *mythos*—eternal or figurative meaning.[56] People could examine printed textual content for themselves, rather than having it interpreted for them orally by an authority figure. Though it took place over centuries, this shift towards

---

[56] See Armstrong (2000) for an extended explanation of *logos* versus *mythos* in the context of contemporary religious fundamentalism.

messages being conveyed in writing (rather than orally) has affected how people regard knowledge.

The belief systems of Medieval Europe changed fundamentally over the next three hundred years, as mechanically printed books and other ideas were propagated. If the printing press as a technology and social catalyst had a tectonic effect, the impact of several *particular* books shook the pre-modern worldview to its foundations.

One secular book with enormous impact was Francis Bacon's articulation of the scientific method. In his treatise *Novum Organum*, (first published in 1620), he contributed to the preeminence of empirically based and falsifiable, rather than authority-based, knowledge. *Novum Organum* demonstrated that knowledge is testable.

Solutions or pieces of knowledge can be tested and shown to be wrong; this new way of laying a brick of knowledge or technique, testing it, and laying the next one on top has been the foundation of knowledge ever since.

Preceded by the first European research universities, scientific societies (such as the Royal Society of London, founded in 1650) were formed, enabling scientists like Isaac Newton to meet with aristocrats and merchants. Eventually, merchants made up two-thirds of the scientific societies, as they sought to apply science to making profits and avoiding risks. Such applied sciences included navigation, cartography, hydraulics, ballistics, and oceanography. The merchants gained social power as they gained economic power. The first cyclopedias were published in the 18th century, and enabled ordinary men and women to find and digest knowledge for themselves.[57]

---

[57] Modernity and an information revolution could be propagated in Europe in part because Europe is physically small. The Dutchman Erasmus could visit St. Thomas More in England for an in-person exchange of ideas. Visits, books, journals, and cor-

Another book that shook Europe was *The Martyrs' Mirror of the Defenceless Christians*, compiled by Thieleman J. van Braght, a Dutch Mennonite pastor, and first published in Dutch in 1660. It told the story of the persecution of Anabaptists, who insisted that their number should consciously choose to enter a religious group, since Anabaptists favor volition in pledging themselves to a particular faith rather than having baptism thrust upon unknowing infants. This account of atrocities also raised questions of why people might kill in the name of religion, and why Anabaptists resisted authority and Catholic, Calvinist, Puritan and other competing monotheistic dogma.

Elevation of the individual and of free will and reason, as well as the pursuit of commerce and worldly wealth, were norms advanced by the Protestant Reformation. The Reformation strengthened the merchant class, which encouraged technological improvements (for profit reasons). These served as the basis for the scientific revolution, which gave birth to the Enlightenment, which invented the idea of progress, which is the central component of modernity (i.e., change for the better over time), which is the very ethos of today's middle class and a crucial foundation of the democratic nation-state.[58]

The scientific method as a new way of solving problems and pursuing goals played a crucial role in the economic transformation of the 15th to 18th centuries. Rationalization of agriculture and enterprise (combined with enclosure of what had been publicly used land in Eng-

---

respondence propagated the ideas of intellectuals—and a questioning stance subsequently permeated the middle class via subscriptions to journals and other printed vehicles.

[58] Admittedly, along with this optimistic perspective, modernity created a problematic requirement in the system of capitalism—the necessity that consumption and production must ever increase. More bushels of wheat, more automobiles, more houses and higher prices for them are necessary for prosperity. The subprime mortgage crisis beginning in 2008 is stark evidence of the pitfalls of this necessity.

land and Western Europe in the mid-18th century) caused real productivity to grow for the first time since humans settled in villages.

The normative shifts of modernity were more transformative even than the informational and cognitive changes it brought. The Greeks had laid the groundwork for confidence in the knowability of the world, pursuit of understanding, and love of knowledge itself (thus *philo – sophy*). Although leaders, scientists, and merchants of the Renaissance and Enlightenment pursued modernity to attain wealth and improvement of material life, they contributed to the creation of a middle class and with it the ideas of human rights, the plebiscite as a basis for government, and the perfectability of earthly society.

Along with a cognitive or paradigmatic shift came a normative shift. People's estimation of what is valuable (the individual person or the common good, for example), how resources should be allocated, what is right and wrong, whether anything can be done about social problems, and how to pursue social justice, all changed.

## The Difference between Modernity and Modernism

Modernity, the historical process, has much to recommend it. At its best, it has offered ways to bring together differing and competing interests to forge agreements to protect the weak, marginalized, unlucky, and even the deviant members of society. When I bare my arms, or speak my mind, or walk past a church to attend a yoga class on Easter Sunday, I am thankful for modernity and that I am free to use my time and direct my energies as I choose.

Modernity brought tremendous measurable benefits. Life expectancy nearly doubled in Europe in the century and a half after 1850. The indisputable beacon of modernity is in all the lives of all the babies who grew to adulthood beginning in the mid-19th century. Infant mortality rates plummeted because mothers and fathers could afford less costly, mass-produced wool socks and blankets, soap to kill germs, and metal pots in which to cook.

Modernity is the term for five centuries of philosophical and social change from the 14th century through the Industrial Revolution. And it is the term we should continue to apply to social problem solving.

Modernism, on the other hand, is an ideology—a logic that is immune to reason. In the Twentieth Century, the very systemization and rationality that people expected would make war obsolete actually allowed weapons and supply lines to consume a staggering number of human lives on the front lines. Death counts were in the tens of millions due to the essentially modern totalitarian impulses to perfect and control society—in the Soviet Union[59], Nazi Germany[60], Cambodia[61], and other totalizing regimes. The toll of modernism is the loss of the sons and daughters—those who lived and those who were never born—as a result of industrially supported violence at Ypres, Verdun, Dresden, Dachau, Hiroshima, Nagasaki, and Tuol Sleng.

World War I was the first, and perhaps the most shocking, betrayal of the promise of modernity. Nearly seven million people—the flower of a continent's youth—died in the Great War in combat alone, and more than twice that many as a result of the war's social effects—famine, disease, accidents, displacement. Fifty to seventy million died in combat in World War II. The silenced springs of 1918 and 1945 were more tragic than any Rachel Carson described.

The American-English poet T.S. Eliot is credited with one of the icons of modernism in literature: his prophetic, sweeping, and nihilistic 1922 poem *The Wasteland*. Eliot's is an early voice of the 20th cen-

---

[59] Under the cult of personality of Josef Stalin.
[60] Unifying the state and the people in the *Reichsfolk*.
[61] Striving toward "perfection" of the agrarian communist utopia.

tury presenting a vision of the future that is not clean, unsullied, and comprehensible, but rather chaotic and ruined. Other writers exploring the excesses of modernism included Franz Kafka, James Joyce, Albert Camus, and Arthur Miller. Miller's play *Death of Salesman* juxtaposes the hyperrationality of capitalism with the protagonist's realization that his aspirations have been polluted and betrayed.

The ideology of modernism, though it has roots in individualism, destroys lives in favor of efficiency, short-term profit, and visions of the perfectibility of human society. Modernism is also the rationale behind the externalization of cost, externalization of pollution, and degradation of life by private interests. This rationale cleverly pushes such cost onto the "commons" (and the commoners), so that they bear the brunt of private profit. Modernism has produced what Thomas Friedman (2008) calls the "sub-prime planet." Elites and grifters are able to maximize utility now for their own advantage, to the later detriment of the unlucky, the gullible, and, eventually, of society as a whole.

Modernity, on the other hand, *has* truly led to the survival of more children, longer and better lives for many, and a sustained flourishing of intellectual and cultural society. Modernism is like a dangerous invasive species that comes to dominate a more diverse and richer social ecosystem, crowding out the valuable meaning-making that is inherent in the conventions of the more traditional world. The liberation of modernity and the calculus of modernism are conjoined twins whose relationship must be understood for us to proceed in a sustainable world with a paradigm that works.

Given the destructive dimension of modernism, where can we find moral credibility? Postmodernism, with its idea of "standpoint" or subjectivity, became the antidote to the totalizing capacity of modernism. Postmodernism argued that the clarity and unity of rational understanding had been an illusion or worse: a power play by dominators and colonizers to seize from the people of non-European cultures what was rightfully theirs.

A great triumph of the scientific method was that it offered a way to test (and legitimate or discard) various explanations for empirical phenomena. However, what it did *not* do was acknowledge or provide a way to "test" intensely different subjective, aesthetic or other psychological "truths." Postmodernism and postcolonialism restored a voice to individuals who felt themselves to be marginalized by modernism's emphasis on homogenization and universalization. Passerin d'Entrèves (1996) expresses postmodernism's response to modernism as the responsibility to *recognize* differences and disagreements. This recognition seems to offer little advice on action based on acknowledgment.

Furthermore, Habermas (1981/1987) asserts that the responsibility to communicate, understand, and cooperate to solve social problems trumps the responsibility to acknowledge differences of perspective or previous mistakes in understanding. Taylor (1994) later explores the philosophical roots of the acknowledgment of diverse groups and comes to the conclusion that only a celebration of the universal human potential in all people and cultural groups *combined with* a culturally-blind, procedurally-oriented (therefore modern) provision of identical rights, can guide diverse societies to meaningfully resolve conflicts and craft social policy.

The problem with Taylor's conclusion is that only one paradigm has a self-correcting mechanism of critique and constitutionalism. In the Beatles movie *Help* (1965), an Anglican priest has a theological discussion with a (farcically fictionalized) Thugee priest—and in the name of mutual tolerance—tries to accommodate the practice of eating the hearts of victims of human sacrifice. This is an absurdly humorous depiction of the moral problems with tolerating fundamentally inhumane practices as cultural idiosyncrasies.

In other words, to discount particularity-blind proceduralism as unfairly biased toward white Anglo-Saxon is to remove a workable tool for those who would craft social justice. Falk, anthologized in An-Na'im, makes this point, saying, "When a government rejects modernization as part of a repudiation of the West, as has been the case with Iran since the Islamic Revolution of 1979, the normative ideology has been narrow and intolerant, denigrating all other cultural traditions represented within the sovereign territory. It should be remembered that one positive feature of Westernization as it has evolved since the Enlightenment is a principled toleration of diverse views, not so much as reflected in group membership but as indirectly validated by including within individual rights discretion as to group identity and cultural affiliation." An-Na'im (1992, 61)

Modernity does need to be less dismissive of traditionality, but it has the *equipment* for bringing diverse players to a table of negotiation. No other system of allocation of political power can make this claim. Conversely, although, postmodernity critiques the (potentially oppressive) certainty of modernity, it doesn't offer an effective program for action, only critique (admitting that I myself argue that language itself is a form of action).

## Modernity as a Property of the Nation-State

Against the backdrop of the Protestant Reformation and increasing reliance on rationality to understand society and power, Thomas Hobbes, David Hume, John Locke, Jean-Jacques Rousseau, Immanuel Kant, and other political theorists turned their attention to the whys and wherefores of government. What is in it for those being ruled? And what is the source of the rulers' legitimacy?

From 1618 until 1648, a generation-long religious war had ravaged Germany and most of the other nations of central Europe. The war led to an agreement that the church of the ruler of each state (rather than a vast theocratic empire centered outside most of those European states) would determine the religious practice of the citizenry. Most political scientists regard the treaties that ended the Thirty Years' War as the beginning of a new institution, the nation-state. In the Treaty of Westphalia, the signatory duchies, cities, and other polities were framed as legal persons. This reveals the era's ascendant rationality and proceduralism—and linguistic expression of these values.

The English monarch Charles I was beheaded in 1649, and Oliver Cromwell became the Lord Protector of the short-lived English Commonwealth. The old system of hereditary privilege and power, particularly as manifested by the Catholic king's assertion of his divine right, was shoved aside to make room for reason and political power based in the plebiscite. This development is one of the first glimpses of the ruthless side of modernity: it eradicates that which is not intrinsically rational and evolved, an invasive species crowding out other modes of thought.[62]

In the Age of Enlightenment, a new picture was advanced to contend with the seeming incompatibility of faith and reason—the deistic picture of God. God the watchmaker created an orderly universe, wound it, and then withdrew from the lives of humans to watch it tick.

---

[62] There's another conversation here, which must be deferred to another day, and that is the consideration of culture and social practices in the ecosystem analogy of politics. In biology, invasive species are adaptable, which may be a good thing, as long as they do not push other species to extinction. Or perhaps even the extinction of dinosaurs is to be welcomed if mammals replace them, but if the entire balance of the ecology (keeping in mind that we are talking about a global political ecology) is thrown off so that no species survives then this is to be prevented.

This compromise is consistent with the perspective of the framers of the American constitution, who generally held a vaguely Protestant, non-literal belief in a transcendent God—indeed, in a very transcendent God—completely removed from the material world, watching but not interfering directly in human affairs. As God the watchmaker receded into the background, political theorists and revolutionaries crafted language to explain the source of political rights of human beings (e.g., nature, a capacity for reason) and their relationship to governmental authority.

Rationality, rationalization of production, industrialization, commoditization of work *and* culture, and the elevation of efficiency to a social value are all part of modernity as it is manifested in the nation-state. As theorized by Anderson (1983/2006), Gellner (1983), Hobsbawm (1962, 1990), and Hobsbawm & Ranger (1983), the nation-state is symbiotic with the Industrial Revolution. The standardization and interchangeability that are part of the industrial ethos of modernity were also manifested in the concept of nation-ness. Progress was a standard template by which any society could be measured. The nationalist independence movements that followed the age of colonialism employed modernity's ideal of interchangeability and standardization of nation-ness so that formerly colonized people could build their own nation-states.

## Suggested Directions of the Modernity of the Nation-State

The meaning of the word "modern" has been problematic since it was first used to refer to art and literature. "Modern" painting and sculpture correspond to "postmodern" literature, in that both reject representation or narrative and involve play, discovery, shock, and rejection of rationality and realism. Modern architecture is unadorned—

its shape depending completely on its function. "Modern" can be used to mean anything from "contemporary" to "technological" to emblematic of society's ills today.

The 16 public intellectuals whose texts I analyzed varied widely in how they addressed the concept of modernity of the nation-state. Some use "modern" and "modernity" as synonyms for developed nations and development, both economic and technological. In this case, the words are intended to distinguish the wealthy West from the rest.

Others use "modernity" simply as a synonym for progress. Some of the public intellectuals use the word to refer approvingly to the achievements of the Western and wealthy world, while others use "modernity" as code for the excesses of capitalism and globalization to be deplored. A few dig into the historical roots I have explored and urge institutions and policies to re-commit to true modernity—that institutions and nation-states comply with their own stated rules. A rarified few have ideas and recommendations for the evolution of modernity, particularly the modernity of the nation-state.

## Modernity as Progress and Prosperity

Most diplomats and statesmen have used "modernity" in its most elementary meaning—technologically advanced, oriented toward progress, or prosperous.

Citizens of postcolonized and struggling countries must cringe when they hear the word "modernity" from Western lips, since it often means, "We have it. And if you had it, you would behave better." This usage dichotomizes cultures into traditional or modern, backward or capable of harnessing technology and being productive. Thomas Friedman uses "modernity" in this sense, although more recently he has explored how to make progress—that is, modernity—more sustainable and equitable and has begun to call for the pursuit of clean energy and for richer (and more wasteful) nations to assist less advanced nations.

Former U.S. National Security Advisor Zbigniew Brzezinski, U.S. Secretary of State Hillary Clinton, former U.S. Secretary of State George Shultz, and the respective presidents of India and Russia, Pratibha Patil and Dmitry Medvedev, all predominantly use the term "modernity" to represent progress to be emulated.

George Mitchell, who brokered peace in Northern Ireland, did so in part with the even-handedness and power sharing of which modernity is capable. In his current role as American special envoy to the Middle East, he has been sent there initially merely to "listen." At the same time, he has made it clear that symmetry must begin with the dismantling of Israeli West Bank settlements and a return to pre-1967 boundaries.[63]

Richard Holbrooke, President Obama's special representative to Afghanistan and Pakistan, has seen that democracy, although often viewed—particularly in the West—as a pillar of the modern nation-state, has problems. "Suppose that elections are free and fair and those elected are racists, fascists, and separatists. That is the dilemma," said the architect of the Dayton Accord that ended the Bosnian Wars. Holbrooke has been an advocate of state building, but with the proviso that the state built must protect vulnerable minorities. Democracy must not be a value in and of itself, but rather a means to social justice, wrapped in limitations of the state and protections of the people.

---

[63] Cohen (2009) has also advocated more "modern," that is, rational (rather than fearful) thinking about the ratcheting up of security measures and territorial buffers that Israel has pursued. Prime Minister Ariel Sharon originally believed that a buffer of land would make Israel safer. But then events revealed that protecting Israel's claim to Palestinian land was creating more problems than it solved. This kind of thinking is what I mean by "modernity" in international relations.

Like Holbrooke, Zakaria has asserted that the modernity of the nation-state must be better than brute majoritarianism—that there must be covenants and authority committed to those covenants in order to protect the citizenry.

Mitchell and Holbrooke, both now re-activated as diplomats in the administration of President Obama, have shown that they know the deeper story. Like other statesmen and world leaders, President Obama is somewhat limited by the need to make his public speeches accessible. His speeches do not dwell on—or even explicitly mention—the historical and philosophical underpinnings of modernity. Nonetheless, it is clear from recent addresses (particularly those given beyond American shores) that, while he is well aware that "modernity" can connote progress, capitalism, and globalization, he also sees the associated indignity and oppression. In this respect, President Obama's approach is consistent with the idea of "mutuality" that Habermas advances (see discussion below).

It seems to me that President Obama also believes that (1) the language we choose in talking about the world's direst problems must have some agreed upon meaning; (2) carefully chosen language *is* a useful tool that can be employed to reach agreements, which can then be implemented; and (3) the nation-state still holds potential for sharing power. All three of these beliefs are unmistakable tenets of modernity.

## Necessary Critiques of Modernity

Ossified modernity can be oppressive, even totalitarian. It is thoroughly modern to believe that society can be perfected and that brutal means to this end are justifiable. It is the modernity of the nation-state that forces one mold onto everyone. At the core, nearly every utopian is a totalitarian, ready to jail, kill or exile the oddballs who don't fit in.

This is evidenced by the paucity of literary and philosophical utopias where the watchword is "live and let live."

One of the problems of petrified modernity as a property of the nation-state is that it is insufficiently resilient, or compassionate, or sustainable. This is why modernism must be wrapped in constitutionalism, as Zakaria explains.

First wave modernity may have degenerated into an anti-humanist ideology, but it also provided contracts—between the state and industry and between the state and citizens—upon which people could rely. Manufacturers expected to be protected by the state, and were expected to provide for the well-being of workers. The advent of globalization has seen the erosion of these implied commitments of corporations to localities and workers. These contracts have now been dismantled in pursuit of the comparative advantage that a given locale might offer in terms of cheaper labor, greater expertise, heightened geographical advantage, or plentiful raw materials. Of the 16 public intellectuals whose texts I considered, critics of failed modernity include Arjun Appadurai, Zygmunt Bauman, and Pepe Escobar.

In Appadurai's view (1996a), modernity is no longer under the control of the nation-state, the institution that compellingly advanced it. Rather, Appadurai says, modernity is now "at large" and whirling out of control, propagated in ways as different and strange as movies exported around the globe and international investment.

Bauman decries what he sees as the failure of modernity in the contexts of emancipation, individuality, time-and-space, work, and community. All of these, but the last in particular, are intertwined with the nation-state and its advancement of modernity. Bauman's overarching point is that the more recent or decadent form of modernity has lost structural integrity (in contrast to an earlier, more solid modernity). In his section on "emancipation," Bauman bemoans the messiness of modernity and the growing rift between the most "emancipated" segment of society ("emancipated" in terms of convenience and comfort) and the most wretched, whether they live in the poorest country or the richest Bauman then decries the savagery of individuality and the loss of community.

Like Giddens (1990) and Albrow (1996), Bauman examines how the openness and serendipity of public space is lost as the gap yawns between rich and poor in the new "liquid" modernity. He laments a reconstruction of time in which anyone can have nearly anything they want when they want it, without aligning themselves with the social time of others. His section on work pursues similar themes found in Harvey (1989)—that work in its earlier manifestation entailed covenants between workers and employers, that workers' lives were expected to consistently improve, and that there were some guarantees of worker protection in their role in a larger, coherent social and governmental system. Bauman, and also Escobar, deplore the narrow, self-interested, commodified modernity as now unstable, unsustainable, or "liquid."

## Discovery and Application of Consistent Rule Sets

Too often, the arguments of the powerful and privileged in the international community have been framed in terms that sound something like, "If only these impoverished and backward people could adopt our methods of modernity, they could have all the prosperity we enjoy." Joseph Stiglitz directly addresses—and blasts—this line of argument in *Globalization and Its Discontents* (2002), where he points out that the markets pushed from richer countries onto poorer ones are anything but free and consistent—that is, based on transparent rule sets in which the ruled are allowed to participate in rule-making. Rather, the already-advantaged nation-states impose produce and processes on fragile emerging economies while selfishly protecting their own national economies.

Thomas P.M. Barnett, formerly a senior strategic researcher and professor at the U.S. Naval War College, uses the word "modern" in the conventional sense—to mean technologically-oriented and reaping the benefits of the Industrial Revolution and contemporary information technology. At the same time, Barnett's more recent emphasis on "rule sets" renders his thinking remarkably consistent with Habermas' argument that society as a whole should pursue a shared understanding of "person," "society," and even "public good," and should negotiate a binding rule set that becomes a kind of operating system for a just and functional social sphere. Presumably, however, the German philosopher would not support Barnett's earlier suggestion that security should be exported to less stable locales, nor would he favor Barnett's state-building proposals. The problem being that when they are imposed from the outside, transplanted governmental arrangements can be expensive, corrupt and unstable. The success stories of nation building in Japan and Germany have yet to be repeated. Emerging nation-states might best be supported by other members of the international community backing off and letting nascent nation-states take responsibility for their own affairs. The important exception being when a nation-state, despite requests from outside, allows itself to be a base from which to attack other parts of the world.

An-Na'im and Annan have also both advocated for modernity in their respective quests for a humane basis for universal ethics and rule sets. Annan has alluded to deeper meanings of "modernity" in addressing the struggle between the West and the traditionality of the Middle East, has attempted to find common ground, such as *ijtihad*, the tradition of independent legal interpretation in the Quran. And Javier Solana has asserted that the best way to protect members of the E.U. and the macroregion is to craft a network of nation-states in which citizens have representation and which function by rule of law.

Though they don't frame it in terms of fulfilling modernity, a number of authors in this group of 16 have written about pursuing social justice through internal consistency and recommitting to transparent rules. One of the most compelling arguments comes from Stiglitz (2003). The former cabinet level advisor to President Clinton asserts that wealthy countries steering the World Bank and W.T.O. are hypocritical in prescribing different rules for developing countries than for "developed" ones. This unfair inconsistency is exacerbated by the fact that U.S. policy makers interpreting modernization theory in the 1960s expected simply to lay the pattern for American and Western economic growth over countries in African, Asia and the Middle East. (Rostow, 1960)

In *The Future of Freedom* (2003), Zakaria makes the related point that the *rules* of the modern nation are not as straightforward as winner-governs-all, in other words, *before* you democratize you had better constitutionalize.

Ignatieff may be most emblematic of the evolution of the modernity of the nation-state: the positions he has taken as a politician and scholar have publicly and visibly evolved over time. Once he strongly advocated for intervention (as in the Iraq war), but he has since taken a far more nuanced position on the pitfalls and exigencies of any nation-state stepping into the affairs of another state. (2006, 59-75)

## Evolving Modernity of the Nation-State

Diplomat Robert Cooper uses "modern" to mean narrowly self-interested and uses "postmodern" to mean cooperative, transparent, and contractually based pursuit of long-term and mutual benefits, rather than brute balance-of-power based actions. Regardless of terminology, Cooper's proposal is notably similar to that advanced by Habermas—a mutually beneficial, negotiated, transparent arrangement of power sharing to ensure stability and security.

What Cooper (2003) calls the "postmodern" nation exemplifies what I would call new, or sustainable, or integrative *modernity*. Charles Taylor suggests the recognition of "multiple modernities," rather than the ham-handed pursuit of one totalizing and oppressive way to run a society or a government. Like Taylor, Fareed Zakaria (2008) points out in his most recent book that the modernity of Europe's shift during the Renaissance and Enlightenment to inquiry, falsifiability, and rationality will not necessarily be the same modernity that develops in the now fastest growing economies of Southeast Asia and some segments of the Middle East. Clearly, as Zakaria notes, the modernity of Dubai, Singapore, and India will not be based on the English language, or any sort of non-religious Protestantism, or Euro-Western cultural predilections. Falsifiability, specifically, is intimidating to many, since no one wants their religious faith or other dearly held ideas "falsified." Still the trend is toward evidence-based practices in many public realms from education to health care. If the public dollar is being spent on an activity or it affects the law, there needs to be a way to tell if it is helping or hurting the situation.

For Jürgen Habermas, modernity is the use of language to deliberate, share power, attain some consensus, and determine the written rule set to which a society must adhere (constitution). At their heart, the tradition and stability of the pre-modern world were based in authority backed up by force. But authority and force cannot drive a globalized, multicultural society, Habermas says in his writing about the "unfinished project of modernity" (Passerin d'Entrèves, 1996; Habermas, 1998). Such force is both ineffective and unjust.

Habermas asserts that a set of workable rules for a diverse, open, free society can only be legitimized by the reason and agency of the plebiscite that is to be bound by those rules. For Habermas, the question is how to identify that rule set. He asserts that modern law, rather than prepolitical moral assertions about the rights of humans, must be the basis of a social contract. This would entail negotiated rights mutually conveyed on members of society by one another.

Old modernity does not intrinsically provide for mutuality, but Habermas says that codified standing in society must be something that people *confer upon one another* in a balancing act of interdependent recognition. There are other authors, such as Axelrod (1984/2006), who explore cooperation through language. However, the potential for cooperation, rather than hopeless misunderstanding, has been gravely tarnished in public perception and as a useful tool in international politics, and needs to be reinvigorated.

## The Unfulfilled Promise of Modernity

An icon of modernization—both as mechanical actuality and metaphor—is the assembly line. Henry Ford witnessed hogs being *disassembled* in the slaughterhouses of Chicago and exported the idea to Motor City. While such techniques and the larger ethos of modernity led to unprecedented prosperity, these concepts and techniques were also used in the machine guns of WWI and gas chambers of WWII, combined with a view of the "purity" of nations that arises from the expected property of nation-state "unity."

In *Multiculturalism* (1994) Taylor conducts a careful discussion of the (modern) growth of proceduralism. He beats a last-minute retreat from universalism, however, saying that rule- and rationality-based political process is itself a kind of biased particularism. His worry is both that perfectly equal treatment of the present does not correct unequal treatment of the past and that certain groups may have concerns for their survival or needs that perfectly equal treatment does not address.

For Abdullahi Ahmed An-Na'im, an avowed Muslim of Sudanese origin, the universalism of the secular nation-state does not compel sameness. It allows for differences. He argues that only a secular state can protect genuine Islamic religious practice. His argument is that theocracy forces a show of devotion, while the choice inherent in separation of church and state ensures that piety will be volitional. His is a classically modern conception of the secular nation-state based on free will, free reason, and sets of rules to contend with differences in the people within the nation-state.

But what is the use in updating so abstract and ethereal a concept as modernity? My answer is that abstract concepts and metaphors are the basis for social policy, for resource allocation, and for the incentives governments provide to encourage citizens to be responsible, productive, prosperous, and (to some extent) self-reliant.

The character of modernity is to test solutions to see if they can be improved. Modernity is *neither* intrinsically ossified nor fundamentally flawed. The mechanical and ideological foundations of the Industrial Revolution are useful, and can be improved somewhat, both in actuality and as metaphors.

In need of updating are the concepts of the assembly line, standardization, one-size-fits all, interchangeability, centralization, totalization, and linearity. Updates of modernity can include phenomena that we already see emerging in the business world, such as flattened organizations, networking, webs of inclusion, polycentralization, just-in-time production, customization, portability, accessibility, transparency, empowerment, and incrementalism.

At their best, applied to government and policy making, these principles will be crucial to harnessing modernity for justice and fundamental social reform. At their worst, they might amount merely to a more elaborate spider web of social control.

# Chapter Eleven. The Archaeopteryx

The task at hand. Understanding globalization. The power of language. Hatching the nation-state.

\*

You more than anyone have the ability to re-imagine the world, and then remake this world.

—President Barack Obama, speaking June 4, 2009 at Cairo University

Richard J. Barnet's (1971) assertion that the nation-state had become a dinosaur (the graphic that the *New York Times* editorial board placed at the top of his essay) was intended to shock policy makers into steering the (American) government into doing what the writer saw as its job. Titled "Farewell to the Nation-State" his editorial decried the waste of resources (that he asserted should have gone to social welfare) on military force in Vietnam.

The nation-state, both as a concept and a verbatim turn of phrase, stays in the background to a remarkable extent, considering how huge an idea it is. When it *is* invoked, it is meant to draw attention to the taproot of modern society and how we see people and power being organized.

Of late, when writers invoke the nation-state they negate it, as a rhetorical device, to assert there is a breakdown in the fundamentals of civilization.

Since the industrial revolution, since the upheavals of two world wars, and during economic busts of the past several generations, many of the world's people have surely struggled and suffered. Yet, it seems to me there *is* a more recent sense that something very new and very big is very wrong. From national dissolutions and civil wars, to protests in Seattle in 1999 over the policies of the W.T.O., to non-states lashing out at nation-states—a number of warning wildfires have conveyed this sense of *koyaanisqatsi*, or life out of balance. Or more precisely, when writers in the public sphere respond to such events, they respond with a rhetoric that says, "See, something is terribly wrong. (The nation-state is breaking down....")

Responding to such discourse, I searched for broad-based perceptions of a postnational world, but I did not find major evidence of such perceptions when a large sample of textual data was examined as a whole. In the texts I reviewed, I found no substantive description of emergent social structures to take the place of the nation-state. Neither did I find much to suggest the rise of anything like the "virtual nations" that I originally postulated, nor was the "globality" predicted by Albrow (1996) strongly corroborated. I think now that the most likely emergent macro social structures (other than the nation-state which I assert is the best we have to work with) may be the macroregional agreements, described by Cooper (2003), that link the functioning of cooperative, transparent, "postmodern" nations.

A member of my dissertation committee, Jim Spickard, mused that perhaps the lack of discourse about something other than the old workhorse of the nation-state was a "failure of imagination." Perhaps this is so. In part, it was pursuit of more creative imaginings of the nation-state that led to this book.

## Understanding Globalization

So as to address how globalization is pushing on the institutions designed for another era, we need to get a better handle on what this

189

term means. Whether the course being taught is contemporary social problems or global news or another subject—I always ask my students what they hear when someone says, "globalization." They frequently admit that it seems to be a buzzword that they don't fully understand, though they hear all the time.

Even while people of high school and college age are involved with globalization in an immediate way via popular culture exponentially individuated on cell phones, iPads, and web 2.0 sites, it seems to them too big and too complicated as a social or political concept. It is too abstract—incomprehensible in its effects beyond their daily lives.

Meanwhile, the words of ordinary, intelligent people on small media and big: National Public Radio, in newspapers, on Facebook, YouTube, and blogs reveal the shared perception of our intensified connectedness. People increasingly *do* have some sense of globalization—that their destinies are entangled with those of distant strangers, and that their actions—particularly when added up—have aggregate effects that matter more than they ever have before.

My students and other members of the public have an inkling that their coffee has traveled thousands of miles; that the oceans have been nearly emptied of the tuna they eat; that their jeans were handed off from some distant, impoverished locale—the cotton grown in an impoverished place, woven into fabric in a semi-poor place, and assembled into a garment in yet a third; that the lights, computers, and cars they use are mostly propelled by fossil fuels pumped out of the ground in some of the most unstable regions and fragile biomes of the world. They have some sense that the vast majority of people eat a handful of rice per day, if they have that much. People do apprehend their mutuality with and dependence on the transnational workers around them— from the landscapers who trim the shrubs of their municipal buildings to the migrant worker who picked the tomatoes in their sandwiches.

What many people lack—including my students, the people on whose doors I have knocked while doing political work, those I have served in soup kitchens, and those whose voices I have read in the newspaper or heard on the radio—is a theoretical framework for thinking about how their jeans got to them, whether the hands that made them ever used a ballot box, if the workers who picked their coffee were protected by occupational health and safety laws or a constitution, or why those who extract or pump the oil they burn might be improvising explosive devices to hasten a new polity of "their own" based on politicized religion or ethnicity.

In order to provide a theoretical context to allow us to think about the connection between that nagging sense in the backs of our minds about of how globalization connects to us and what to *do* about it, I have laid out in this book four abstract characteristics of the nation-state that I believe are being re-thought in scholarly work and *should* be re-thought in public discourse.

Nearly every one of the 16 public intellectuals whose work I cite might also be called a globalization theorist of one kind or another. Four categories of *non*-state-centered theories–(1) cultural clashes, (2) the global economy, (3) return to empire, and (4) large-scale cooperation and other efforts to manage globalization—offer a way to better understand public intellectuals' recommendations for the evolution of nation-state properties.

## The Task at Hand

After reviewing the various conjectures about the patterns to be found in a recent explosion of nation-state shifts, I assert that the change taking place is both more reassuring and more revolutionary than the predictions that were first made about changing world order after the end of the Cold War, such as de-territorialization of nations or the de-nationalizing of world order.

The task at hand is to study the work of thinkers who are trying to understand what is going with world order and to employ what ideas they share so that we can formulate a plan of action. If their language gives some direction for the evolution of the properties of the nation-state then that may help us find our way as globalization is squeezing our most important institutions.

How can we navigate our increased interdependence using the institutions we have to work with? One solution may come through the universalism sought by An-Na'im, Annan, and Taylor, or a society based on transparency and interdependence such as Cooper praises, or the re-energizing of reason and language that Habermas espouses, or the rule sets and symmetry advocated by Friedman, Barnett, and Cohen. These ideals all hold enormous potential to rehabilitate the nation-state.

As I was realizing that the nation-state was the institution to which writers issued a call to do a better job—not some other metanational nor unnamed emergent structure—I found intimations of four ways the nation-state *could* be updated to better cope with globalization. This book is an attempt to pursue those intimations as well as my own proposal to correct internal contradictions created by sovereign, bounded, supposedly ancestrally or ethnically defined, modern states as they are crashing headlong into globalization. Specifically, I recommend that we all work together for the following changes in the nation-state:

1. Conception and implementation of conditional rather than absolute nation-state sovereignty;

2. Surgical precision in defining nation-state boundaries so that we can and do block weapons of mass destruction, disease, human traf-

ficking and other potentially catastrophic bodily and moral threats—while softening the moral panic and persecution committed in the fight against marijuana and other drugs, and against Mexicans and other immigrants who merely want to participate in economy of the wealthy world. Yes, nation-states should cooperate across boundaries to pursue murderers, but making (American) drug laws more consistent and rational will support not impede this effort.

3. What Habermas calls "constitutional patriotism"—a renewed pride that citizens take in the particularity-blind proceduralism and justice of which the nation-state is capable. *This* patriotism should be the emphasis, rather than accident of ancestry, ethnicity or religious identity.

## The Power of Language

A central premise of this book is that language matters. The language used by the 16 public intellectuals and other theorists and thinkers is the best tool we have to first understand those global connections and to bring that understanding back to the things we say and the choices we make. That doesn't mean that it is a perfect tool. Language is not reality unto itself, but it is the most compelling way that people both convey their perception of reality and shape reality through the process of communicating. The language that describes social structure has already shaped our political reality, and it can help compel society's continued maturation.

In the newspaper editorials and letters to the editor that I studied, I saw related families of ideas. My findings for the dissertation were that modernity and the nation-state remained central to the editorial writers' recommendations, but that they also perceived declining fulfillment by nation-states of sovereignty, boundedness, attribution at the national level, protection of and provision for citizenry, and national

193

unity. I also saw intimations that sovereignty, boundedness, "unity," and modernity needed to be re-thought for the nation-state to survive as a functioning structure.

The op-ed contributors who wrote the 555 newspaper texts—many now dead, some living and still writing—moved me to tears in their hopes for world government in early 1946, their globalist exhilaration at the Apollo 11 moon shot, and their sick shame at revelations of Bush-era American interrogation techniques. Again I was reminded of the underlying principle that guided my entire search for re-imagined nation-state properties: Language matters. What we say shapes what we do as members of a society.

## The Next Evolution of the Nation-State

The nation-state is being pressured from both above and below. Pressure from above comes from macroregional or global organizations that arrive at agreements or set goals the nation-state must then implement and fund. Pressure from below comes from small groups that can incite an autoimmune response in the nation-state, prompting it to falter in its commitment to procedures, review of policies, and inhibition of governmental coercion.

Joseph Stiglitz writes about how nation-states must be better coordinated to achieve what they were designed to do while addressing some problems that can only be solved at a global level. He writes:

> Economic globalization has outpaced political globalization. We have a chaotic, uncoordinated system of global governance without a global government, an array of institutions and agreements dealing with a series of problems, from climate change to international trade and capital flows. Finance ministers discuss global finance matters at the I.M.F., paying little heed to how their decisions affect the environment or global health. Environmental ministers may call for

something to be done about global warming, but they lack the resources to back up those calls. (2006, 21)

Stiglitz goes on to lay out a program of (in particular) environmental targets for positive goals and taxes for drains on the total system
that are to be discouraged, like carbon emissions. He states the need
for a process of global problem solving built on a foundation of public
confidence and political will.

There is a need for macroregional or even global organizations to
better steer the agendas and efforts of nation-states, but these organizations continue to be funded and legitimated by nation-states. More
importantly, the large-scale coordination of this global layer of governance will falter without a reinvigoration of the nation-state. Such
large-scale organizations lack the capacity of negotiation, representation, and self-limitation that the nation-state possesses. In short, the
nation-state has a basis in people that the E.U., NATO, the W.T.O.
and the World Bank will never have.

This project of reinvigoration can be commenced by appreciating
the mythological dimension of the nation-state and making use of that
mythology in a positive way. It still has ideals that compel people and
can help to rally the resources that are, as Stiglitz notes, lacking at the
next higher level. Furthermore, one value in talking about reenergizing
the nation-state in the abstract is that doing so emphasizes the characteristics and functions that many nation-states have in common. There
are vast differences among members of the G-20 or the 192 members of
the UN. But if we concentrate on what the U.S. and Russia or France
and India have in common—as nation-states—it may facilitate the cooperation necessary for nation-states to survive the throes of globalization.

The nation-state is not a dinosaur—nearing extinction and hope-
lessly overrun by faster, hotter creatures. The archaeopteryx is a more

apt metaphor for the nation-state. By the measure of our short lives, the nation-state is ancient: it has endured for a dozen generations. Along with its crimes, it has allowed people to soar, to build projects, and to feed their neighbors in a way unattainable by previous civilizations. It is the best political achievement of its fossil age, an evolving species, and perhaps incubating still better things to come.

# GLOSSARY

**Bretton Woods Agreement**—The financial arrangement crafted by Allied nations in Bretton Woods, New Hampshire, in 1944 at the end of WWII. Political scientists refer to the Bretton Woods Agreement as the "Westphalia" of the global economy—a turning point marking the shift from discrete nation-state economies to a boundary-less system set up so that nation-state economies could flow into one another with fewer barriers. Bretton Woods established the International Bank for Reconstruction and Development (IBRD; now one of five institutions in the World Bank Group) and the International Monetary Fund (*I.M.F.*). The IBRD and the *I.M.F.* began to operate in 1946 after countries ratified the Bretton Woods Agreement.

**Culture**—A set of tools and patterns, including objects, moral values and life patterns, that people acquire and adapt as members of social groups. Culture has two main dimensions: Material culture consists of things such as food, tools, clothes, etc., while non-material culture consists of abstractions or ideas. The cognitive component consists of knowledge and belief systems–fundamental frameworks of how a macro group believes that the world works. The normative component of non-material culture consists of moral values, ethics, and etiquette, i.e., the "right way to behave" in both large and small ways. The symbolic component consists of signs, symbols, and forms of language—the building blocks of meaning.

**Globalization**—increased economic interdependence and integration among the national economies and people of the world caused by greater speed and volume of people, raw materials, finished goods, information, and forms of money crossing nation-state boundaries. Two main causes of globalization since WWII are the Bretton Woods Agreement, which unified the economies of 44 Allied nations at the end of WWII (and subsquent consolidation into one global economy through the activites of metanational organizations like the E.U., I.M.F, World Bank and W.T.O.) and the instantaneous telecommunication enabled by Internet-based and other networks. The unification of the global economy and instantaneous communication have enabled the flow of investments, revenues, finished goods, raw materials, personal messages, and cultural products (such as films, music and even video statements by terrorists taking "credit" for attacks), as well as the movement of human beings across nation-state boundaries.

**Macro-social structures**—The largest organizations into which human beings form themselves. Here, this term is principally used to refer nation-states, but it can include empires, metanational organizations, other cooperations among nation-states or other polities, the financial networks of the world, and large multinational corporations.

**Metanations** or **metanational projects (used interchangeably)**— Organizations, such as the United Nations (U.N.), North Atlantic Treaty Organization (NATO), World Trade Organization ( W.T.O.), World Bank, or European Union (E.U.), that are created by agreements among nation-states, thereby becoming rule makers for the rule makers. The Greek word "meta" meaning "above" or "beyond" implies complete dominion by such organizations; indeed, public intellectuals writing soon after the founding of the U.N. anticipated only world government within a decade. However, the reality is that nation-states desire some degree of sovereignty, and metanations have functioned as steering committees or advisory boards to facilitate agreement and cooperation by nation-states on monetary policy, trade, development, security, environmental goals, etc. Nation-states appear to remain the dominant macro social structure.

Some see a major problem with so-called metanations in that they have neither been sufficiently akin to democratic republics nor have they been sufficiently "meta," that is above or able to compel their members. The authority and funding of the United Nations, European Union, etc. derives from nations. They are more like "meta-instrumentalities" or "meta-bureaucracies" and awkwardly functioning ones at that, with many of the problems of nation-states and fewer of their covenants or procedural advantages. See also the footnote in chapter seven on H.A.L. Fisher's history of the League of Nations.

This point must be made in combination with the observation that all metanations, while containing the word "nation" have so far been fundamentally undemocratic in operation. The supposedly representational structure of the United Nations is a problematic distortion of democracy in nation-states, with gross imbalances in the number of human beings represented by a "vote" in that intenational body.

**Nationalism**—Nationalism can mean the project of setting up a separate nation-state by (usually ethnically allied) political factions within a larger nation or it can mean subnational resistance without the requisite cohesion to ever set up a new, stable nation-state. The major proponents of the modernist perspective in political science— Anderson (1983/2006), Gellner (1983), and Hobsbawm (1962)—use "nationalism" to mean nation-state projects, which were for their era mostly decolonization and the subsequent tailoring of the nation-state to the purposes of formerly colonized countries, e.g., Thailand or Kenya. The most valuable recent theory on what it takes for nationalism to form countries that can hold together comes from Roeder (2007). He explains how what he calls administrative "segment-states" are necessary for new nation-states to succeed as independent polities. However, in the texts that I read from the *New York Times*, *Times of India* and *Daily Gleaner*, "nationalism" was used not to suggest building a new nation, but rather pulling away or trying to pull away (almost always on grounds of ethnic separatism) from existing central powers. Yet a third meaning of "nationalism" is the study of nations by political scientists. Because of the confusion inherent in the term, I am very sparing in its use.

**Nation-State**—A technical term used by political scientists to refer to the people and cultural patterns of a nation in confluence with the land that the people occupy, along with the state that governs the people and controls that land. "Nation" means inhabitants and cultural patterns; "State" means territory and government. The four come together to refer to the institution that had been dominant in world order for approximately three centuries.

**Paradigm**—A framework of interconnected ideas—a particular perspective on reality and how the world works. This word was central to *The Structure of Scientific Revolutions* by Thomas Kuhn (1962). In his seminal book about how new ideas become accepted, which Kuhn intended to apply to "hard" sciences like physics, the main idea is that the sciences do not advance Truth with a capital "T"—rather, waves of dominant ideas are slowly discredited and replaced by new paradigms. (For example, Einstein's theory of relativity led to an overhaul of Newtonian physics. In turn, Heisenberg's uncertainty theory required modifications to some of Einstein's more certain and predictable assumptions regarding particle position and velocity.) In this book, I use the term "Paradigm" to mean "theory" or explanatory emphasis in the political and social sciences.

**Public Sphere**—Jürgen Habermas (1962/1991, 1992) is the author of the notion of the "public sphere." He originally described it as any physical meeting place where people could talk about social problems and areas of public policy that need to be corrected. This idea has since expanded to include "spaces" made possible by the Internet, such as blogs, forums, and bulletin boards. In such spaces, people are free to express ideas and they may also change their opinions, be influenced by one another, and cooperate on plans of action, particularly political action. The public sphere is a social space between the "private sphere" and the "sphere of public authority," which commands and controls people and allocates public resources (sometimes using economic or legal force). Relevant to this book, an important part of the theory of the public sphere is that governmental power is legitimated by listening to and engaging with the public sphere. Therefore, influence in the public sphere influences the government of any given nation-state and the evolution of macro social structures, such as nation-states or cooperation between nation-states and macroregional metanations.

**Social Construction**—A reality based on shared agreement, such as money or marriage. Paper money can be traded for goods or services because people behave collectively as though it has worth, therefore it does. People are perceived as having a particular social standing after undergoing a marriage ceremony because there is shared agreement that their social standing has changed. A social construction may have a thin basis in physical or biological reality but has *social reality* based on predominant perception and behavior. A social construction is real because people behave as though it is real.

**Social Structure**—Association into which people organize themselves (and the abstract labels that social scientist apply to such associations) such as "family," "nation-state," "community," etc. The important idea is that these structures derive their reality from people's collective believe that they exist and matter.

**Social Problem**—A phenomenon that is publicly recognized as measurably predominantly negative in its impact on people. To be called *social* problems, such negative phenomena must have aggregate or social—rather than psychological, medical or other merely individual—causes. There is a range of theoretical perspectives on what should be considered a social problem (and therefore be addressed by intervention by the nation-state or other governmental entities). Social problems can be seen a "disease" of the "social body," or a breakdown in the "machine" of society. These two are the two earliest metaphors for understanding social problems. Critical theory on social problems (with its roots in Marxist analysis of class conflict) is also very valuable in its consiseration of whose has power and who controls resources regarding the underlying causes of any given social problem. A positivist approach to social problems demands that a moral panic or a claim that something is a "social problem" is substantiated by defining that problem, measuring its negative overall effect on society, and substantiating the value of proposed interventions by the community or government. See Rubington and Weinberg (2003) for an overview of seven theoretical perspectives on social problems.

**Sovereignty**—The property attributed to the nation-state in theorizing the meaning of the Peace of Westphalia of 1648 that ended the Thirty Years' War in what is now Germany. For the purposes of that resolution, "Sovereignty" was framed as noninterference by one nation-state in the internal affairs of another.

**Virtual Nation**—Political factions that do not possess the same confluence of power with defined territory that conventional nation-states do. They are "virtual" in the sense that they operate where they can and are tied by ideology, but do not manifest a number of the properties of other social structures. The "cellular" social structures described by Appadurai (2006) to which I refer in chapter nine are conceptually related to virtual nations.

Authors who have written about entities that might be called virtual nations have largely come from military-strategic or scholarly backgrounds. In *Brave New War*, strategist John Robb talks about attacks on civilians and infrastructure by what he refers to as "virtual networks of grievance" (2007, 3-41), meaning subnational entities that share a sense of having been wronged. Roeder (2007) also describes such alliances of shared grievances and says that they desire land and a nation-state of their own. However, Robb asserts that some groups, such as al Qaeda, seek to destabilize the nation-state not in hopes of carving out a nation-state of their own, but to seize the power that the nation-state currently holds. Van Creveld explores the extent to which the nation-state is an "abstract organization" (1999, 179, 183, 304); his inquiry is consistent with Anderson's (1983/2006) idea that the nation-state is imagined (not actual or material). Van Creveld predicts the emergence of additional abstract organizations beyond nation-states' reach to meet the needs of citizens. Eriksen (2007) also looked at what he calls "abstract communities" (2007, 6), both nation-states and other kinds of allegiances created by Internet-based communication.

Other scholars have examined the phenomenon of citizens clinging to national identity even after their nation-states have dissolved or ceased to function. These disrupted or diasporic communities may cleave more closely to their nation-state or ethnic group than they do to the government of the territory in which they find themselves. Scholars writing on this phenomenon have proposed that new forms of citizenship are emerging in new, virtual social structures.

This program of first identifying the expected functions of the dominant political institution will seem quixotic to some. My hope is that laying out the well-documented ideal of what is still the most powerful abstraction in the world will allow us to re-imagine more consciously and conscientously.

NIMBLE BOOKS LLC

# Texts by the 16 Public Intellectuals

An-Na'im, Abdullahi Ahmed, ed. 1992. "Toward a cross-cultural approach to defining international standards of human rights: The meaning of cruel, inhuman, or degrading treatment or punishment." In *Human Rights in Cross-Cultural Perspectives: A Quest for Consensus*. Philadelphia: University of Pennsylvania Press.

An-Na'im, Abdullahi Ahmed. 2002. "Speech to the World Humanist Congress at Noordwijkerhout, July 4. www.iheu.org/node/196 (accessed May 19, 2009).

An-Na'im, Abdullahi Ahmed and Francis Deng. 2006. "Self-determination and unity: The case of Sudan." *Respect, Sudanese Journal for Human Rights, Culture and Issues of Diversity.* Issue 4 (Nov.)

An-Na'im, Abdullahi Ahmed. 2008. *Islam and the Secular State: Negotiating the Future of Shari'a.* Cambridge: Harvard University Press.

Annan, Kofi. 1999a. "No government has the right to hide behind national sovereignty in order to violate human rights." *The Guardian*, April 7.
www.guardian.co.uk/world/1999/apr/07/balkans.unitednations (accessed Apr. 3, 2009).

Annan, Kofi, 1999b. "The dialogue of civilizations and the need for a world ethic." Lecture at the Sheldonian Theatre, Oxford, June 28.

Annan, Kofi. 1999c. "Two concepts of sovereignty." *The Economist* 352(8137):49-50.

Annan, Kofi. 2000/2004. "The role of the state in the age of globalisation." *The Globalization Reader*, eds. John Boli and Frank Lechner 2nd ed. Hoboken: Wiley-Blackwell.

Annan, Kofi. 2002a. "Trade and aid in a changed world." *New York Times*, March 19. www.nytimes.com/2002/03/19/opinion/trade-and-aid-in-a-changed-world.html?scp=4&sq=&st=nyt (accessed Apr. 3, 2009).

Annan, Kofi. 2002b. "Celebrating the birth of a nation." *Christian Science Monitor*, May 7. www.csmonitor.com/2002/0507/p11s01-coop.html (accessed Apr. 3, 2009).

Annan, Kofi. 2003. "Challenge for all is to manage interdependence." Address on Interdependence Day, Philadelphia, Dec. 9. www.un.org/News/Press/docs/2003/sgsm8871.doc.htm. (accessed May 20, 2009).

Annan, Kofi. 2005. "Billions of promises to keep." *New York Times*, Apr. 13. www.nytimes.com/2005/04/13/opinion/13annan.html?_r=1&scp=3&sq=&st=nyt (accessed Apr. 3, 2009)

Annan, Kofi and Allan Thompson. 2007. *The Media and the Rwanda Genocide*. Ann Arbor: Pluto Press.

Annan, Kofi. 2008. Address on receiving the MacArthur Award for International Justice in New York City, March 20.

Appadurai, Arjun. 1993. "Patriotism and its futures." *Public Culture* 5(3):411-429.

Appadurai, Arjun. 1996. *Modernity at Large: Cultural Dimensions of Globalization*. Minneapolis: University of Minnesota Press.

Appadurai, Arjun. 1996. "Sovereignty without territoriality: Notes for a postnational geography." In *The Geography of Identity,* ed. Patricia Yaeger. Ann Arbor: University of Michigan Press.

Appadurai, Arjun, ed. 2001. *Globalization.* Durham: Duke University Press.

Appadurai, Arjun. 2006. *Fear of Small Numbers: An Essay on the Geography of Anger.* Durham: Duke University Press.

Barnett, Thomas P. M. 2004. *The Pentagon's New Map: War and Peace in the Twenty-first Century.* New York: Putnam Publishing Group, Inc.

Barnett, Thomas P. M. 2005. *Blueprint for Action: A Future Worth Creating.* New York: Putnam Publishing Group, Inc.

Bauman, Zygmunt. 1976. *Socialism, The Active Utopia.* London: Allen and Unwin.

Bauman, Zygmunt. 1989. *Modernity and the Holocaust.* Ithaca: Cornell University Press.

Bauman, Zygmunt. 1998. *Globalization: The Human Consequences.* New York: Columbia University Press.

Bauman, Zygmunt. 2000. *Liquid Modernity.* Malden, MA: Polity Press.

Bauman, Zygmunt. 2004. *Wasted Lives: Modernity and its Outcasts.* Cambridge: Polity Press.

Brzezinski, Zbigniew. 1997. *The Grand Chessboard: American Primacy and Its Geostrategic Imperatives.* New York: Basic Books.

Brzezinski, Zbigniew. 2005a. "The dilemma of the last sovereign." *The American Interest Magazine Online* 1(1). www.the-american-interest.com/article.cfm?piece=56.

Brzezinski, Zbigniew. 2005b. "The danger of a 'lonely American war'." Keynote Address at the Middle East Institute's 59th Annual Conference, Nov. 17. www.saudi-us-relations.org/articles/2005/ioi/051117-brzezinski-mei.html (accessed Jan. 19, 2008).

Brzezinski, Zbigniew. 2007a. "Failure risks devastating consequences." *New York Review of Books*, Nov. 8. www.nybooks.com/articles/20750

Brzezinski, Zbigniew. 2007b. *Second Chance: Three Presidents and the Crisis of American Superpower*. New York: Perseus Books.

Brzezinski, Zbigniew. 2007c. Address to the World Affairs Council in Philadelphia, Apr. 19. [In connection with *Second chance: Three presidents and the crisis of American Superpower*].

Brzezinski, Zbigniew, Brent Scowcroft and David Ignatius. 2008. *America and the World: Conversations on the Future of American Foreign Policy*. New York: Basic Books.

Brzezinski, Zbigniew. 2009. "What Next for NATO? Toward a Global Security Web." *Foreign Affairs*. 88(5): 2-20. September/October.

Cooper, Robert. 1996. *The Post-Modern State and the World Order*. London: Demos.

Cooper, Robert. 2002. "The post-modern state." In *Re-Ordering the World: The Long-Term Implications of September 11*, ed. Mark Leonard. London: Foreign Policy Centre. Originally appeared in *The Guardian*, Apr. 7, 2001.

Cooper, Robert. 2003a. "Democracy cannot be imposed on a nation by force of arms." *The Independent*, Aug. 1. www.independent.co.uk/opinion/commentators/robert-cooper-democracy-cannot-be-imposed-on-a-nation-by-force-of-arms-588596.html

Cooper, Robert. 2003b. "Civilise or die." *The Guardian*, October 23. www.guardian.co.uk/politics/2003/oct/23/eu.foreignpolicy (accessed July 17, 2009).

Cooper, Robert. 2003c. *The Breaking of Nations: Order and Chaos in the 21st Century*. New York: Atlantic Books.

Cooper, Robert. 2005. Statement to U.S.EU-POLMIL Conference: ESDP Goals and Ambitions in Brussels, Dec. 10.

Cooper, Robert. 2006a. "The mystery of development." *The Prospect*, February. www.prospect-magazine.co.uk/article_details.php?id=7295 (accessed July 17, 2009).

Cooper, Robert. 2006b. "War and democracy." *The Prospect*, June. www.prospect-magazine.co.uk/article_details.php?id=7456 (accessed July 17, 2009).

Cooper, Robert and Robert Kagan. 2008. "Is democracy winning? Is the world reverting to a struggle between great powers? Or is the democratising spirit of 1989 still alive?" *The Prospect*, May. http://www.prospect-magazine.co.uk/article_details.php?id=10165 (accessed July 17, 2009).

Cooper, Robert. 2009. Press statement as Director-General for External and Politico-Military Affairs, General Secretariat of the Council of the E.U. in answer to 'What are the E.U.'s strengths and weaknesses in crisis response?' June 3. www.dailymotion.com/video/x9k125_robert-cooper-eu-council-general-se_news (accessed July 17, 2009).

Escobar, Pepe. 2001. "Get Osama! Now! Or else." *Asia Times Online*, Aug. 30. http://www.atimes.com/ind-pak/CH30Df01.html

Escobar, Pepe. 2005. "The new French revolution." *Asia Times*, May 28. http://www.atimes.com/atimes/Front_Page/GE28Aa01.html. (Accessed May 20, 2009).

Escobar, Pepe. 2006. Globalistan: *How the Globalized World is Dissolving into Liquid War*. Ann Arbor: Nimble Books.

Escobar, Pepe. 2007. *Red Zone Blues: A Snapshot of Baghdad During the Surge*. Ann Arbor: Nimble Books.

Escobar, Pepe. 2009. *Obama Does Globalistan*. Ann Arbor: Nimble Books.

Escobar, Pepe. 2009. "Beyond the summit: Pepe Escobar on Obama-Bush in Afghanistan-Pakistan." *Asia Times Online*, May 7. http://enduringamerica.com/2009/05/07/beyond-the-summit-pepe-escobar-on-obama-bush-in-afghanistan-pakistan/

Friedman, Thomas L. 1999/2000. *The Lexus and the Olive Tree: Understanding Globalization*. New York: Farrar, Straus and Giroux.

Friedman, Thomas L. 2005. "Just shut it down." *New York Times*, May 27. www.nytimes.com (accessed May 7, 2008).

Friedman, Thomas L. 2006a. "The kidnapping of democracy." *New York Times*, July 14. www.nytimes.com (accessed Apr. 28, 2008).

Friedman, Thomas L. 2006b. "Order versus disorder." *New York Times*, July 21. www.nytimes.com (accessed Apr. 28, 2008).

Friedman, Thomas L. 2005/2006. *The World Is Flat: A Brief History of the 21st Century*. New York: Farrar, Straus and Giroux.

Friedman, Thomas L. 2008. *Hot, Flat, and Crowded: Why We Need a Green Revolution - and How it Can Renew America*. New York: Farrar, Straus and Giroux.

Habermas, Jürgen. 1962/1991. *The Structural Transformation of the Public Sphere: An Inquiry into a Category of Bourgeois Society*. Trans. Thomas Burger with the assistance of Frederick Lawrence. Cambridge: MIT Press.

Habermas, Jürgen. 1969/1971. *Knowledge and Human Interests*. Trans. Jeremy Shapiro. Boston: Beacon Press.

Habermas, Jürgen. 1981/1984. *The Theory of Communicative Action: Reason and the Rationalization of Society*, Vol. 1. Trans. Thomas McCarthy. Boston: Beacon Press.

Habermas, Jürgen. 1985/1987. *The Theory of Communicative Action: Lifeworld and System: A Critique of Functionalist Reason*, Vol. 2. Trans. Thomas McCarthy. Boston: Beacon Press.

Habermas, Jürgen. 1986. *Autonomy and Solidarity: Interviews with Jurgen Habermas*. Ed. Peter Dews. London: Verso.

Habermas, Jürgen. 1987. *The Philosophical Discourse of Modernity*. Trans. Frederick Lawrence. Cambridge: MIT Press.

Habermas, Jürgen. 1996. "The European nation-state—Its achievements and its limits. On the past and future of sovereignty and citizenship." In *Mapping the Nation*, ed. Gopal Balakrishnan. New York: Verso.

Habermas, Jürgen. 1992. *Further Reflections on the Public Sphere*. Cambridge: MIT Press.

Habermas, Jürgen. 1998a. *The Inclusion of the Other: Studies in Political Theory*. Trans. Ciaran Cronin and Pablow De Greiff. Cambridge: MIT Press.

Habermas, Jürgen. 1998b. *Between Facts and Norms: Contributions to a Discourse Theory of Law and Democracy*. Trans. William Rehg. Cambridge: MIT Press.

Habermas, Jürgen. 2001. *The Postnational Constellation: Political Essays*. Trans. Max Pensky. Cambridge: MIT Press.

Habermas, Jürgen. 2003. "Fundamentalism and terror." In *Philosophy in a Time of Terror: Dialogues with Jürgen Habermas and Jacques Derrida,* ed. Giovanna Borradori. Chicago: University of Chicago Press.

Ignatieff, Michael. 1984. *The Needs of Strangers*. New York: Viking Penguin Inc.

Ignatieff, Michael. 1993. *Blood and Belonging: Journeys into the New Nationalism*. London: BBC.

Ignatieff, Michael. 1997. *The Warrior's Honor: Ethnic War and the Modern Conscience*. New York: Henry Holt and Company.

Ignatieff, Michael. 2000. *The Rights Revolution*. Toronto: House of Anansi Press.

Ignatieff, Michael. 2001. *Human Rights as Politics and Idolatry*. Princeton: Princeton University Press.

Ignatieff, Michael. 2003. *Empire Lite: Nation-building in Bosnia, Kosovo and Afghanistan*. London: Minerva. http://empirelite.ca/ First published in *New York Times Magazine* as "The Burden" on Jan. 5.

Ignatieff, Michael. 2004a. *The Lesser Evil: Political Ethics in an Age of Terror*. Princeton: Princeton University Press.

Ignatieff, Michael. 2004b. "The terrorist as auteur." *New York Times*, November 14. www.nytimes.com/2004/11/14/movies/14TERROR.html?scp=5&sq =michael%20ignatieff&st=cse (accessed June 9, 2009).

Ignatieff, Michael, ed. 2005a. *American Exceptionalism and Human Rights*. Princeton: Princeton University Press.

Ignatieff, Michael. 2005b. "The uncommitted." *New York Times Magazine*, Jan. 30. www.nytimes.com/2005/01/30/magazine/30WWLN.html?scp=2& sq=michael%20ignatieff&st=cse

Ignatieff, Michael. 2005c. "Who are Americans to think that freedom is theirs to spread?" *New York Times Magazine*, June 26. www.nytimes.com/2005/06/26/magazine/26EXCEPTION.html?sc p=6&sq=michael%20ignatieff&st=cse

Ignatieff, Michael. 2006. "Human Rights, Power and the State." In *Making States Work: State Failure and the Crisis of Governance*, eds.

Simon Chesterman, Michael Ignatieff, and Ramesh Thakur. New York: United Nations University Press.

Ignatieff, Michael. 2007. "Getting Iraq wrong." *New York Times Magazine*, Aug. 5. www.nytimes.com/2007/08/05/magazine/05iraq-t.html?scp=3&sq=michael%20ignatieff&st=cse (accessed June 9, 2009).

Shultz, George P. 1985. "New realities and new ways of thinking." *Foreign Affairs* 63(4):705-721.

Shultz, George P. 1990. "A chance for some serious diplomacy in the Middle East," *Washington Post*, March 6, 23.

Shultz, George P. 1993. *Turmoil and Triumph: My Years as Secretary of State*. New York: Scribner's.

Shultz, George P. 2006. Lecture at Preventive Force Conference, Princeton University. March 15-16.

Shultz, George P. and James A. Baker III. 2007a. "Why the 'law of the sea' is a good deal," *The Wall Street Journal*, Sept. 26, A21.

Shultz, George P., William J. Perry, Henry A. Kissinger, and Sam Nunn. 2007b. "A world free of nuclear weapons." *The Wall Street Journal*, Jan. 4, A15. http://www.fcnl.org/issues/item.php?item_id=2252&issue_id=54

Solana, Javier. 1998. "Securing Peace in Europe." Speech at the Symposium on the Political Relevance of the 1648 Peace of Westphalia. www.nato.int/docu/speech/1998/s981112a.htm   (Accessed Feb. 2, 2008).

Solana, Javier. 2003. "The transatlantic rift: U.S. leadership after September 11." *Harvard International Review* 24(4):62-65.

Solana, Javier (Preface) and Nicole Gnesotto (Ed.) 2004. *E.U. Security and Defence Policy-The First Five Years (1999-2004)*. Paris: E.U. Institute for Security Studies.

Spickard, James V. 2007. "'Religion' in global culture: New directions in an increasingly self-conscious world." In *Globalization, Religion, and Culture,* eds. Peter Beyer and Lori Beaman. Boston: Brill.

Spivak, Gayatri Chakravorty. 1988. "Can the subaltern speak?" In *Marxism and the Interpretation of Culture*, eds. C. Nelson and L. Grossberg. Urbana: University of Illinois Press. Spivak, Gayatri Chakravorty. 1998. "Love, cruelty, and cultural talks in the hot peace." In *Cosmopolitics: Thinking and Feeling beyond the Nation,* eds. P. Cheah and B. Robbins. Minneapolis: University of Minnesota Press.

Spivak, Gayatri Chakravorty. 1999. *A Critique of Postcolonial Reason.* Cambridge: Harvard University Press.

Spivak, Gayatri Chakravorty. 2004. "Terror: A speech after 9-11." *Boundary 2, 31*(2):81–111.

Stiglitz, Joseph. 2003. *Globalization and Its Discontents.* New York: W.W. Norton and Co.

Stiglitz. Joseph. 2006. *Making Globalization Work.* New York: W.W. Norton and Co.

Taylor, Charles. 1989. *The Sources of the Self: The Making of Modern Identity.* Cambridge: Harvard University Press.

Taylor, Charles. 1991. *The Ethics of Authenticity*. Cambridge: Harvard University Press.

Taylor, Charles. 1994. *Multiculturalism: Examining the Politics of Recognition*. Ewing: Princeton University Press.

Taylor, Charles. 2004. *Modern Social Imaginaries*. Durham: Duke University Press.

Zakaria, Fareed. 2005. "How to stop the contagion." *Newsweek*, Aug. 1.

Zakaria, Fareed. 2003. *The Future of Freedom: Illiberal Democracy at Home and Abroad*. New York: W.W. Norton and Company.

Zakaria, Fareed. 2008. *The Post-American World*. New York: W.W. Norton and Company.

# OTHER REFERENCES

Albrow, Martin. 1996. *The Global Age: State and Society beyond Modernity*. Stanford: Stanford University Press.

Ali, Tariq. 2000. *Masters of the Universe: NATO's Balkan Crusade*. New York: Verso.

Ali, Tariq. 2002. *The Clash of Fundamentalisms: Crusades, Jihads and Modernity*. New York: Verso.

An-Na'im, Abdullahi Ahmed. See **Texts by the 16 Public Intellectuals**.

Anderson, Benedict. 1983/revised 2006. *Imagined Communities: Reflections on the Origins and Spread of Nationalism*. New York: Verso.

Annan, Kofi. See **Texts by the 16 Public Intellectuals**.

Appadurai, Arjun. See **Texts by the 16 Public Intellectuals**.

Armstrong, Karen. 2000. *The Battle for God*. New York: Ballantine Books.

Aslan, Reza. 2008. *How to Win a Cosmic War: God, Globalization, and the End of the War on Terror*. New York: Random House.

Auerbach, Erich. 1946/1953. *Mimesis: The Representation of Reality in Western Literature*. Trans. Willard Trask. Princeton: Princeton University Press.

Axlerod, Robert. 1984/2006. *The Evolution of Cooperation*. New York: Basic Books.

Barnett, Thomas P.M. See **Texts by the 16 Public Intellectuals**.

Bauman, Zygmunt. See **Texts by the 16 Public Intellectuals**.

Besteman, Catherine and Hugh Gusterson. 2005. *Why America's Top Pundits Are Wrong*. Berkeley: University of California Press.

Bielefeld, Ulrich. 1993. "Conversation with Janina Bauman and Zygmunt Bauman." Trans. David Roberts. Mittelweg 36. www.pucp.edu.pe/ridei/pdfs/Ulrich_Bielefeld_Conversation_with_Janina_Bauman_and_Zygmunt_Bauman.pdf (accessed Apr. 3, 2009).

Bobbitt, Philip. 2002. *The Shield of Achilles: War, Peace, and the Course of History*. New York: Anchor Books.

Bull, Hedley. 1977. *The Anarchical Society: A Study of Order in World Politics*. New York: Columbia University Press.

Brzezinski, Zbigniew. See **Texts by the 16 Public Intellectuals**.

Calinescu, Matei. 1987. *Five Faces of Modernity*. Durham: Duke University Press.

Cavallar, Georg. 1999. *Kant and the Theory and Practice of International Right*. Cardiff: University of Wales Press.

"Charter of the United Nations." 1945. Ratified June 26. www.un.org/en/documents/charter

Chaucer, Geoffrey. Ca. 14th century, earliest extant printing 1467. "The Wife of Bath's Prologue and Tale." Trans. www.courses.fas.harvard.edu/~chaucer/teachslf/wbt-par.htm

Cooper, Robert. See **Texts by the 16 Public Intellectuals**.

Eriksen, Thomas Hylland. 2007. "Nationalism and the Internet." *Nations and nationalism*. 13(1):1-17.

Escobar, Pepe. See **Texts by the 16 Public Intellectuals.**

Fairclough, Norman. 2001. *Language and Power*. 2nd ed. Essex, England: Pearson Education Limited.

Fassihian, Dokhi, Jean-Jacques Damlamian, Priya Patel, and Ted Piccone. 2007. Human rights council report card. Washington, DC: U.N. Democracy Coalition Project. www.freedomhouse.org/template.cfm?page=366&year=2007 (accessed Apr. 30, 2008).

Foster, Charles R., ed. 1980. *Nations Without a State*. New York: Praeger.

Friedman, Thomas. See **Texts by the 16 Public Intellectuals.**

Geertz, Clifford. 2000. "The world in pieces: Culture and politics at the end of the century." In *Available light: Anthropological Reflections on Philosophical Topics*, ed. Clifford Geertz. Princeton: Princeton University Press.

Gellner, Ernest. 1983. *Nations and Nationalism*. Oxford: Blackwell.

Gellner, Ernest. 1997. *Nationalism*. London: Weidenfeld and Nicolson.

Gerdes, Louise, ed. 2006. *Rogue Nations*. Detroit: Greenhaven Press/Thomson Gale.

Giddens, Anthony. 1990. *The Consequences of Modernity*. Stanford: Stanford University Press.

Gilder, George. 2000. *Telecosm: How Infinite Bandwidth Will Revolutionize our World.* New York: The Free Press.

Gleditsch Kristian Skrede and Michael D. Ward. 1999. "Interstate system membership: A revised list of the independent states since 1816." *International Interactions* 25:393-413. http://privatewww.essex.ac.uk/~ksg/statelist.html (accessed July 7, 2008).

Gross, Terry. 2001. "Onion editors regroup following Sept. 11." Interview with editor Rob Siegel and writer Todd Hanson of *The Onion, Fresh Air,* NPR, Oct. 4. www.npr.org/templates/story/story.php?storyId=1130750 (accessed July 15, 2009).

Gross, Terry. 2009. "Covering Iran without a press pass." Interview with *New York Times* journalist Roger Cohen, *Fresh Air*, NPR. July 14. www.npr.org/templates/story/story.php?storyId=106555883 (accessed July 15, 2009).

Guibernau, Montserrat. 1999. *Nations without States: Political Communities in a Global Age.* Cambridge: Polity Press.

Guggenheim, David, dir. 2006. *An Inconvenient Truth: A Global Warning.* Los Angeles: Paramount Vantage/Paramount Classics.

Habermas, Jürgen. See **Texts by the 16 Public Intellectuals.**

Hardt, M. and A. Negri. 2004. *Multitude: War and Democracy in the Age of Empire.* New York: Penguin Press.

Harlow, Harry F. 1959. "Love in Infant Monkeys." *Scientific American* 200 (June).

Harvey, David. 1989. *The Condition of Postmodernity: An Enquiry into the Origins of Cultural Change*. Cambridge: Blackwell.

Harvey, David. 2003. *The New Imperialism*. London: Oxford University Press.

Hirst, Paul. 2001. *War and Power in the 21st Century: The State, Military Conflict and the International System*. Malden: Polity.

Hobbes, Thomas and Edwin Curley. 1994, fp 1668. *Leviathan: With Selected Variants from the Latin Edition of 1668*. Indianapolis: Hacket Publishing Company.

Hobsbawm, Eric. 1962. *The Age of Revolution: 1789–1848*. New York: Random House.

Hobsbawm, Eric and Terrence Ranger, eds. 1983. *The Invention of Tradition*. Cambridge: Cambridge University Press.

Hobsbawm, Eric. 1990. *Nations and Nationalism since 1780: Programme, Myth, Reality*. New York: Cambridge University Press.

Hofstadter, Douglas R. and Daniel C. Dennett. 1981. *The Mind's I: Fantasies and Reflections on Self and Soul*. New York: Basic Books.

Hume, David. 2002, fp. 1741. *Essays and Treatises on Several Subjects*. New York: Thoemmes Continuum.

Huntington, Samuel. 1996. *The Clash of Civilizations: Remaking of World Order*. New York: Touchstone.

Ignatieff, Michael. See **Texts by the 16 Public Intellectuals.**

Jarecki, Eugene, Writer and dir. 2005. *Why We Fight*. Documentary film. Los Angeles: Sony Classics.

Johnson, Chalmers. 2000. *Blowback: The Costs and Consequences of American Empire,* 2nd ed. New York: Holt and Co.

Johnson, Chalmers. 2004. *The Sorrows of Empire: Militarism, Secrecy and the End of the Republic.* New York: Holt and Co.

Johnson, Chalmers. 2006. *Nemesis: The Last Days of the American Republic.* New York: Holt and Co.

Jouvenel, Bertrand de. 1957. *Sovereignty; an Inquiry into the Political Good.* Trans. J. F. Huntington. Chicago: University of Chicago Press.

Kant, Immanuel. 1971, fp. 1784. "Idea for a universal history from a cosmopolitan perspective." In *Berlinische Monatsscrift,* Kant's political writings, ed. Hans Reiss. Cambridge: Cambridge University Press. Also yale-press.yale.edu/yupbooks/excerpts/kant_perpetual.pdf

Kaplan, Robert. 1994. *The Coming Anarchy: Shattering the Dreams of the Post Cold War.* New York: Random House.

Kaplan, Robert. 2005. *Imperial Grunts: The American Military on the Ground.* New York: Random House.

Kierkegaard, Søren. 1844/1957. *The Concept of Dread.* Trans. Walter Lowrie. Princeton: Princeton University Press. Also http://evans-experientialism.freewebspace.com/kierkegaard.htm

Kierkegaard, Søren. 1843/1941. *Fear and Trembling.* Trans. Walter Lowrie. Also http://www.whitenationalism.com/etext/fear.htm

Knoke, William. 1996. *Bold New World: The Essential Road Map to the 21st Century.* New York: Kodansha International.

Kreijen, Gérard. 2004. *State Failure, Sovereignty and Effectiveness.* London: Oxford University Press.

Kuhn, Thomas. 1962. *The Structure of Scientific Revolutions.* Chicago: University of Chicago Press.

Kundera, Milan. 1984. *The Unbearable Lightness of Being.* New York: Harper and Row.

Kunstler, James. 2005. *The Long Emergency: Surviving the Converging Catastrophes of the Twenty-First Century.* New York: Grove/ Atlantic, Inc.

Lentner, Howard. 2004. *Power and Politics in Globalization: The Indispensable State.* New York: Routledge.

Leo, John. 1993. "Rights talk: The impoverishment of political discourse." U.S. News and World Report. June 28.

Lewis, Bernard. 1998. *The Multiple Identities of the Middle East.* New York: Schocken Books.

Lewis, Bernard. 2002. *What Went Wrong? The Clash between Islam and Modernity in the Middle East.* New York: Perennial.

Lewis, Bernard. 2003. *The Crisis of Islam: Holy War and Unholy Terror.* New York: Modern Library.

Lincoln, Abraham. 1861. First Inaugural Address. http://www.historyplace.com/lincoln/inaug-1.htm (accessed July 27, 2009).

Lincoln, Abraham. 1863. Gettysburg Address. http://www.historyplace.com/lincoln/gettys.htm (accessed July 27,

2009). Locke, John. 2008, fp. 1690. *Second Treatise of Government.* New York: Barnes and Noble.

Loewen, James. 1995. *Lies My Teacher Told Me: Everything Your American History Textbook Got Wrong.* New York: Touchstone.

Lukács, Yehuda. 1992. "A new conception of sovereignty." In *The Israeli-Palestinian Conflict: A Documentary Record,* ed. Y. Lukács. Cambridge: Cambridge University Press.

Mamdani, Mahmood. 2009. *Saviors and Survivors: Darfur, Politics, and the War on Terror.* New York: Pantheon Books.

McLuhan, Marshall. 1962. *The Gutenberg Galaxy: The Making of Typographic Man.* Toronto: University of Toronto Press.

McLuhan, Marshall. 1964. *Understanding Media: The Extensions of Man.* New York: McGraw-Hall.

Memmi, Albert. 1965. *The Colonizer and the Colonized.* Boston: Beacon Books.

Merriam, Charles Edward. 1999. *History of the Theory of Sovereignty since Rousseau.* Clark: Lawbook Exchange.

Milton, John. 1668. *Paradise Lost.* www.gutenberg.org/etext/20 (accessed June 9, 2009)

Mongia, Radhika. 2007. "Historicizing state sovereignty: Inequality and the form of equivalence." *Comparative Studies in Society and History* 49(2):384–411.

Moynihan, Daniel Patrick. 1993. *Pandaemonium: Ethnicity in International Politics.* London: Oxford University Press.

Mumford, Lewis. 1967. *Technics and Human Development.* New York: Harvest/HBJ.

Naím, Moises. 2005. *Illicit: How Smugglers, Traffickers and Copycats Are Hijacking the Global Economy.* New York: Doubleday.

Naisbitt, John. 1982. *Megatrends: Ten New Directions Transforming Our Lives.* New York: Warner Books.

Naisbitt, John. 1994. *Global Paradox: The Bigger the World Economy, the More Powerful Its Smallest Actors.* New York: William Morrow and Company.

Nock, Albert J. 1935. *Our Enemy, the State.* New York: William Morrow and Company.

Obama, Barack. 2009a. Speech at Cairo University. Associated Press. www.google.com/hostednews/ap/article/ALeqM5gkyWk2MK7xe Dw2b1jPhFS6KsvPegD98K2EOG0  This URL did not work (June 4, 2009)

Obama, Barack. 2009b. Speech at Town Hall in Strasbourg, France. *Washington Post,* Apr. 3. www.washingtonpost.com/wp-dyn/content/article/2009/04/03/AR2009040301519.html

Passerin d'Entrèves, Maurizio. 1996. "Introduction." In *Habermas and the Unfinished Project of Modernity,* ed. Maurizio Passerin d'Entrèves. Cambridge: MIT Press.

Paul, Thazha Varkey, G. John Ikenberry and John Hall. 2003. *The Nation-State in Question.* NJ: Princeton University Press.

Quandt, William. 2005. *Peace Process: American Diplomacy and the Arab-Israeli Conflict since 1967*. Berkeley: University of California Press.

Redd, Adrienne. 2009a. *Examining Public Discourse for Perception of a Postnational World*. Doctoral diss., Fielding Graduate Univ. http://gradworks.umi.com/33/50/3350593.html

Redd, Adrienne. 2009b. *Obama in Strasbourg: Crossroads of Social Time*. Posted at http://crittjarvis.com/category/adrienne-redd/

Redd, Adrienne. 2009c. "Perception of Social Structures in Public Discourse 1946-2008." *Journal of the Washington Academy of Sciences* 95(3).

Rejali, Darius. 2007. *Torture and Democracy*. Princeton: Princeton University Press.

Renan, Ernest. 1994, fp. 1882. *Qu'est-ce Qu'une Nation?* Leiden, Netherlands: Academic Press Leiden. www.nationalismproject.org/what/renan.htm

Responsibility to Protect. 2001. "Report of the International Commission on Intervention and State Sovereignty." www.iciss.ca/report2-en.asp (accessed July 7, 2009).

Robb, John. 2006. "Nation-states, market-states, and virtual-states." *Global Crime* 7(3–4):351–364.

Robb, John. 2007. *Brave New War: The Next Stage of Terrorism and the End of Globalization*. Hoboken: John Wiley and Sons.

Roeder, Philip. 2007. *Where Nation-States Come From: Institutional Change in the Age of Nationalism.* Princeton: Princeton University Press.

Rosecrance, Richard. 1996. "The rise of the virtual state." *Foreign Affairs* 75(4):45–61.

Rosecrance, Richard. 2000. *The Rise of the Virtual State: Wealth and Power in the Coming Century.* New York: Basic Books.

Rostow, W. W. (1960). *The Stages of Economic Growth: A Noncommunist Manifesto.* New York: Cambridge University Press.

Rousseau, Jean-Jacques. 1968, fp 1762. *The Social Contract.* Trans. M. Cranston. New York: Penguin Classics.

Rubington, Earl and Martin S. Weinberg. 2003. *The Study of Social Problems: Seven Perspectives.* New York: Oxford University Press.

Rummel, Rudolph J. 1997. *Death by Government.* Rutgers: Transaction Publishers. Statistics, description of methods and figures from the book at www.hawaii.edu/powerkills/NOTE5.HTM

Rydgren, Jens. 2007. "The power of the past: A contribution to a cognitive sociology of ethnic conflict." *Sociological Theory* 25(3):225–244.

Skocpol, Theda. 1979. *States and Social Revolutions: A Comparative Analysis of France, Russia, and China.* New York: Cambridge University Press.

Said, Edward. 1979. *Orientalism.* New York: Vintage Books.

Sadowski, Yahya. 1998. *The Myth of Global Chaos: Bosnia and Myths about Ethnic Conflict.* Washington, DC: Brookings Institute Press.

Sassen, Saskia. 1991. *The Global City.* Princeton: Princeton University Press.

Sassen, Saskia. 1994. *Cities in a World Economy.* Newbury Park: Pineforge Press.

Sassen, Saskia. 1996a. *Losing Control? Sovereignty in an Age of Globalization.* New York: Columbia University Press.

Sassen, Saskia. 1996b. "Rebuilding the Global City: Economy, Ethnicity and Space." In *Representing the City: Ethnicity, Capital and Culture in the 21st Century Metropolis,* ed. A. King. London: Macmillan.

Sassen, Saskia. 1998. *Globalization and Its Discontents: Essays on the New Mobility of People and Money.* New York: The New Press.

Sassen, Saskia. 2006. *Territory, Authority, Rights: From Medieval to Global Assemblages.* Princeton: Princeton University Press.

Saxe, John Godfrey. 1968. "The blind men and the elephant." In *The Golden Treasury of Poetry*, 12th edition, ed. Louis Untermeyer. New York: Golden Press.
http://en.wikisource.org/wiki/The_Blindmen_and_the_Elephant

Shakespeare, William. 1882. *King Lear*, a new variorum edition, ed. Horace Howard Furness. New York: Lippincott.

Shultz, George. See **Texts by the 16 Public Intellectuals**.

Smith, Anthony. 1971/1983. *Theories of Nationalism.* New York: Harper and Row.

Smith, Anthony. 1996. *Nationalism and the Historians: Mapping the Nation.* New York: New Left Books.

Smith, Anthony, and John Hutchinson. 1995. *Nationalism*. New York: Oxford University Press.

Solana, Javier. See **Texts by the 16 Public Intellectuals**.

Soros, George. 2000. *Open Society: Reforming Global Capitalism*. New York: Public Affairs.

Soros, George. 2002. *On Globalization*. New York: Public Affairs.

Spickard, James V. 1999. "Origins of Universal Declaration of Human Rights." Unpublished chapter. http://newton.uor.edu/FacultyFolder/Spickard/WebArticles.htm (accessed Apr. 17, 2009)

Stiglitz, Joseph. See **Texts by the 16 Public Intellectuals**.

Sullivan, Michael. 2004. *American Adventurism Abroad: 30 Invasions, Interventions, and Regime Changes since World War II*. Westport: Praeger.

Taylor, Charles. See **Texts by the 16 Public Intellectuals**.

Toffler, Alvin and Heidi Toffler. 1993. *War and Antiwar: Making Sense of Today's Global Chaos*. New York: Warner Books.

Toffler, Alvin. 1995. *Creating a New Civilization: The Politics of the Third Wave*. Atlanta: Turner Publishing.

Tomlinson, John. 1999. *Globalization and Culture*. Chicago: University of Chicago Press.

Treaty of Westphalia: Peace Treaty between the Holy Roman Emperor and the King of France and their Respective Allies. 1648. Avalon Project: Documents in law, history and diplomacy. New Ha-

ven: Yale Law School.
http://avalon.law.yale.edu/17th_century/westphal.asp (accessed Apr. 17, 2009).

van Creveld, Martin. 1999. *The Rise and Decline of the State.* New York: Cambridge University Press.

Weber, Max. 1948. *From Max Weber: Essays in Sociology,* ed. H.H. Gerth and C. Wright Mills. Trans. H. H. Gerth and C. Wright Mills. New York: Routledge.

Weber, Max. 1968. *Economy and Society: An Outline of Interpretive Sociology*, Ed. Guenther Roth and Claus Wittich. Trans. Berkeley: University of California Press.

Weber, Max. 1984. "Legitimacy, Politics and the States." In *Legitimacy and the State*, ed. W. Connolly. New York: New York University Press.

Zakaria, Fareed. See **Texts by the 16 Public Intellectuals**.

# SELECTED OPINION-EDITORIAL TEXTS AND INTERVIEWS

Agarwal, Chandra. 1968. "Cooperation in space." *New York Times*, Dec. 24, 22.

Aub, B. (1992, June 16). Insidious and sinister form of constitutional reform. *The Daily Gleaner*, p. 6.

Barnet, Richard, J. 1971. "Farewell to the nation-state." *New York Times*, June 19, 27.

Cohen, Roger. 2008a. "A change to believe in." *New York Times*. Feb. 21. www.nytimes.com/2008/02/21/opinion/21cohen.html

Cohen, Roger. 2008b. "The global rose as social tool." *New York Times*.

Cohen, Roger. 2009. "Israel, Iran and fear." *New York Times*. Apr. 20. www.nytimes.com/2009/04/20/opinion/20iht-edcohen.html

Friedman, Thomas. See **Texts by the 16 Public Intellectuals**.

*Daily Gleaner*. 1973. "Israeli hijacking." August 16, 10.

Hacker, Andrew. 1964. "What's the mainstream? Who is in it?" *New York Times*, Sept. 6, SM5.

Mojsilovic, Julijana. 1992. "Serbs tell a bitter story of war; Militiamen besieging town say West does not understand." *Washington Post*. Aug. 4, A11.

*New York Times*. 1950a. "The Eritrean knot." July 16, E8.

*New York Times.* 1950b. "Solution for Eritrea." Nov. 28, 29.

*New York Times.* 1963. "World peace through law." June 29, 22.

*New York Times.* 1968. "America, come home." April 6, 39.

*New York Times.* 1992. "Silence Serbia's big guns." July 22, A18.

*New York Times.* 2009. "President Obama's press briefing." June 23. www.nytimes.com/2009/06/23/us/politics/23text-obama.html?_r=2&pagewanted=all (accessed June 26, 2009).

Thwaites, Daniel. 2001. "The unthinkable can happen." *Daily Gleaner.* Sept. 14, A4.

*Times of India.* 1948. "Monstrous failure." May 13, 6.

*Times of India.* 1955. "A challenge to the U.N." Sept. 2, 8.

*Times of India.* 1960. "The Congo mutiny." July 11, 6.

*Times of India.* 1960. "The Congo." Aug. 11, 6.

*Times of India.* 1969. "On the moon." July 22, 8.

*Times of India.* 1974. "A sad end." Aug. 2, 8.

*Times of India.* 1982. "As bad as the Nazis." June 15, 8.

*Times of India.* 2001. "Paradox of America." Sept. 13, 10.

# CREDITS

1. Archaeopteryx from *Encyclopedia Britannica* (1911).

2. "Cracked Egg" by Bob Hires (2010).

3. "Citadel of Emesa" by Louis Francois Cassas (ca. 1786).

4. Indian Elephant from *Encyclopedia Britannica* (1911) via Wikimedia.

5. "Enduring Tree" by Adrienne Redd (2009).

6. "Mouth" by Teresa Westkaemper (ca. 1992).

7. Photograph of Sovrano coin (undated)

8. "Pill bug lateral view" by Harriet Richardson. *Isopods of North America* (1905).

9. Photograph of Moon from Edupics (undated).

10. "Eye" by David Kanoa Helms (ca. 1996).

11. "Egg as Flower Bud" by Adrienne Redd adapted from *Laughable Lyrics* by Edward Lear (1877).

Cover design by Bob Hires. Interior design by Bob Hires, W F. Zimmerman, and Adrienne Redd.

www.ingramcontent.com/pod-product-compliance
Lightning Source LLC
Chambersburg PA
CBHW070809300326
41914CB00078B/1917/J